BEEN OUTSIDE

BEEN OUTSIDE

Adventures of Black Women, Nonbinary,
and Gender Nonconforming
People in Nature

EDITED BY **Amber Wendler and Shaz Zamore**
FOREWORD BY **Carolyn Finney**

**MOUNTAINEERS
BOOKS**

MOUNTAINEERS BOOKS is dedicated to the exploration, preservation, and enjoyment of outdoor and wilderness areas.

1001 SW Klickitat Way, Suite 201, Seattle, WA 98134
800-553-4453, www.mountaineersbooks.org

Printed in Canada
Distributed in the United Kingdom by Cordee, www.cordee.co.uk

26 25 24 23   1 2 3 4 5

Copyeditor: Lorraine Anderson
Design and layout: Jen Grable
Cover and interior illustrations: Simone Martin-Newberry
In several stories, names and/or identifying characteristics have been changed to preserve the privacy of some individuals.

Library of Congress Cataloging-in-Publication Data is on file for this title at https://lccn.loc.gov/2023002412. An ebook record is available at https://lccn.loc.gov/2023002413.

Mountaineers Books titles may be purchased for corporate, educational, or other promotional sales, and our authors are available for a wide range of events. For information on special discounts or booking an author, contact our customer service at 800-553-4453 or mbooks@mountaineersbooks.org.

Printed on 100% recycled and FSC-certified materials

ISBN (paperback): 978-1-68051-592-3
ISBN (ebook): 978-1-68051-593-0

An independent nonprofit publisher since 1960

To the unnamed adventurers who came before us—Black, Indigenous, and other melanated peoples—and shaped the Outside.

———

To our families and outdoor mentors for nourishing our love for the Outside.

———

And to the (young) Black adventurers to come—may you experience an abundance of joy, safety, and accomplishment Outside.

CONTENTS

Foreword by Carolyn Finney **9**
Introduction: Black in Nature **11**

HOW WE ARRIVED

22 Why I Endure / **Dr. Alex Moore**

32 Tragedy before Triumph / **Dr. A. Bashir**

41 Nature, the Perfect Therapist / **Sheridan Alford**

52 Discovering Seasonal Lee / **Leandra Taylor**

59 Return to Sender / **Dakota Lane**

62 Flying Free: Adventures of a Science Cyclist / **Dr. Karine A. Gibbs**

ALL IN

72 They're Just Activities / **Natasha Smith**

76 An Evolving Adventure / **Amber Wendler**

83 A Home in Climbing / **Sidney Woodruff**

91 Out Here / **Dr. Shaz Zamore**

100 Twirling in Nature / **LeeLee James**

WALKING ANCESTRAL PATHS

110 Together We Turn / **Avani Skye Fachon**

116 Dreams of Home / **Dr. Tanisha M. Williams**

122 The Joy and Persistence of the Black
Fisher Tradition / **Camille Mosley**

131 You Should See Me Now / **Xorla Seyram Ocloo**

138 Afro, Sweet Afro / **Boluwatife Olawale**

GROWING TOGETHER

148 Breaking Cycles of Trauma / **Dr. Samniqueka Halsey**

157 Black Women in Nature, Black Women and Nature / **Joelle K. Jenkins**

159 Zion Train / **Kelly GreenLight Thomas**

165 Just Like Me / **Sharon Dorsey**

175 The (Un)written Rulebook / **Jasmin Graham**

185 All I Ever Needed / **Dr. Tiara Moore**

Acknowledgments **192**

References and Resources **193**

FOREWORD

Carolyn Finney

I fell in love with traveling when I was twenty-seven years old. I still have my first backpack—the one I took around the world, that kept me company when I got lost on Mount Kenya, that I carried on the Everest trail in Nepal; that pack took me to the back of the beyond and then some. It was kind of plain, gray and black with aluminum bars, with my blue sleeping bag strapped to the outside. While the bag became worn around the edges over the years, it remained sturdy and strong—not unlike me (mostly). In all my solo traveling in the late 1980s to the mid-2000s, I only once saw someone who looked like me.

You can find a million reasons not to go. Personally, I was tired of being driven by my fear—of being told I wasn't good enough by a country that couldn't see me fully, by my broken heart that wanted to belong somewhere, anywhere. I read hundreds of stories about people climbing mountains, crossing deserts, studying primates, and sailing seas. And while I couldn't find any written by people who looked like me, I wanted some of *that*. I was (and still am) curious and excited to know the world beyond my own skin. Because it isn't just a "Black thing"; it's a human thing—to be in the world and of the world in service to something greater. My dreams needed room to breathe. What better place to do that than outside—with the oceans, mountains, trees, animals, and other people that call this earth home.

Last summer, I had the privilege of being an in-house author at a camp in Denali National Park, sharing my stories with guests. On the way there in an electronics store at the Newark airport, I got into a lighthearted conversation with a young Black man with good-natured, contagious energy. When he asked me where I was traveling, I smiled and said, *"Alaska!"* His eyes widened, "Alaska? *Why are you going there?"* What he was really asking was, *Why would you go to a place where there are hardly any Black people? What are you going to do there? Will you be okay?* I leaned in and whispered, "To tell them about Black people." He responded, "Yes—you need to do that—*good luck!"*

I was once like this young man, navigating the fear, the tension between what-you-know-to-be-true with the potential for change. As it happened, I was the only Black-identified person among dozens of staff and visitors that week. But I got to lie on the tundra in near solitude, to see the mountain when I woke up every morning, to explore the edges of my thoughts and heart with people from around the country in a sublime setting. Was I emotionally and physically challenged? *Absolutely.* Would I do it again? *In a hot minute.*

In a recent *New York Times* article about the rarity of seeing a green comet, writer Shannon Hall explained how "clumps of dust and frozen gases" from the edges of the solar system are jolted by "gravitational agitations sometimes that push them toward the sun" transforming them into "gorgeous cosmic objects." That's how I see these stories in *Been Outside.* The authors cultivate and escalate the very possibilities of who they can be with an honesty and clarity that comes from being knocked about inside and out, and still choosing to lean into a life that can ultimately transform you. Like a chorus of "yes" to a world that has said "no" once too often, these voices are defiant, joyous, vulnerable, unapologetic, badass, and simply gorgeous. You don't need any special equipment to pick up what they're throwing down—just an open mind and heart.

They remind me: We walk. We study. We bike. We hike. We swim. We draw. We listen. We climb. We dream. We love. We hold multitudes. We seek to know ourselves in a world that calls our names, too, and we are all in. Will you join us?

INTRODUCTION: BLACK IN NATURE

Welcome, Black people and people who love us. Welcome, curious adventurers of worlds both internal and external. We adventurers explore to expand our knowledge, stoke sublime feelings, and discover new perspectives. In that spirit, this collection of stories centers field research expertise and the unique extremes of outdoor adventure in tales of fun, whimsy, and joy in nature. *Been Outside* showcases the outdoors beyond the skewed projections of mainstream norms and practices and describes the often-elided relationships Black people have with wilderness. With our histories following diasporic routes, we embrace a broader definition of "Outside," which makes room for our authentic niches in the outdoors to be explored and celebrated. We share with you tender stories, braced with the kind of vulnerability and pride that many experience in outdoor adventures.

As we collected stories and themes, we began to ask the same questions as our foreword author, storyteller Carolyn Finney. Who influences nature? Who goes outside? Who defines the expert? Pondering these questions felt like picking at damaged wallpaper, bit by bit revealing a papered-over heritage. As these questions nagged and pulled, we found boundless treasures, ancestral knowledge in intimate stories, and the birth of a verdant future cradled in poems. The history and practices of

Black women and Black nonbinary, gender nonconforming people are born from generations of exploration, brilliance, and community, and, of course, a shared love of nature. We have been outside.

WHO ARE WE?

The writers who have contributed to this collection come from many walks of life. At first, we focused our search for contributors in the science, technology, engineering, and mathematics (STEM) fields, the professional circle we know best. But no person, and certainly no Black person, is any one thing. Many of the contributors are scientists or engineers and also expert photographers, singers, and devoted parents. Still others are athletes and artists, spiritual leaders and hobby carpenters. We pursue knowledge of the natural world in a multitude of ways: through science, recreation, creativity, stewardship, and self-discovery. We are children of nature, born of and for the earth. We are the living dreams of our ancestors, each working to heal the losses that surviving lineages endure. (And we do so with panache and audacious hope.)

As with all Black communities, we have a diverse and rich heritage. We are African, Indigenous, Latine, and Caribbean; non-binary, transgender, and gender nonconforming people and women. Narratives of gender equality and queer experiences are often dominated by the white voice, so our stories become like the gentle shush of Appalachian woods, or the faint flutter of a hummingbird during the dawn chorus: stillness is often required to hear them. In times of discrimination and triumph alike, we are naively pressured to choose a single identity. (Was it a Black win? Was it a transphobic slight?) For guidance, we listen for the voices of those who came before us. Feminist author and poet Audre Lorde said, "There is no such thing as a single-issue struggle because we do not live single-issue lives." Similarly, there is no such thing as a single-identity win because we celebrate wins as a community. And although we come together in victory as we do in grief and solidarity, no Black group is a monolith. Instead of speaking for entire peoples, we shine a light on the intersections within Blackness and offer readers a trailhead of sorts for any explorer—Black or non-Black, man or gender minority. After all, **everyone** is welcome outside.

AN EXCLUDED HISTORY

We *been* Outside. We stand on the shoulders of giants, but how far down are we encouraged to look? Those who are lauded as "the first adventurer" are usually the first white, male, or European to achieve that goal. For example, the first person who claimed to have continuously hiked the entire two-thousand-some miles of the Appalachian Trail was a white American author, Earl Shaffer, who completed the trek in 1948. Books have been written about his journey, and nonprofit foundations have been established to celebrate his life and writings. The Smithsonian holds one of his handwritten journals and the boots he used for the walk. We celebrate his journey with our peers; it was certainly no easy feat!

One of the contributors to this book, Sidney Woodruff, has pointed out that the wide regard for Shaffer's story leads many people to think that no one ever walked such a journey in those woods before him. White supremacy declared these hiking routes new and waiting to be conquered, and also claimed Shaffer as the first. As Woodruff notes in her essay on rock climbing, signs at every turn on the Appalachian Trail offer whitewashed Civil War history. The history of the land that preceded whiteness was overwritten and forgotten.

A century before Shaffer's journey, an estimated one hundred thousand Indigenous people were forcibly removed from their homes and, in a prolonged tragedy, walked a comparable distance on the Trail of Tears, which overlapped modern-day portions of the Appalachian Trail. In that same period and for decades afterward, one hundred thousand captive Black people escaped the brutalities of slavery by traveling the Underground Railroad, whose many routes coincided with much of the AT.

Time and again, Black and Indigenous people continuously walked, hiked, and swam many of the same stretches of land as Shaffer and other celebrated greats. And like Shaffer, these melanated travelers shared the desire to achieve an impossible feat and arrive safely. Should we applaud only the people who had the privilege to travel the land for fun? Is it just to overlook the people who made the same journey by necessity or force? With this book, we demonstrate the practice of including in our outdoor histories the captive, the forcibly removed, and those fleeing true despair. In so doing, we bravely acknowledge the ugly parts of our history that continue to affect our lives to this day. We applaud the climate migrants traveling, often on foot, from South America to the southern US border. We honor the unnamed captive Black women who braided seeds into other Black people's hair, ensuring ecological and culinary practices would be preserved in the uncertain future. This encompassing celebration decenters whiteness and begins to dismantle racism in the outdoors in the United States.

And so we challenge you, adventuresome reader. When you think of outdoors experts, broaden who comes to mind. Include environmentalists with disabilities, like Harriet Tubman, who identified trees to make the journey along the Underground Railroad at least eighteen times. Thank the Black and Indigenous stewards who meticulously tended land so we could enjoy classic American dishes like pecan pie. Tip a hat to the unnamed captive Black cowboys, who were forced to herd cattle and taught "pioneers" their skill. We challenge you to reflect on the work of Wangari Maathai, a Kenyan woman who founded the Green Belt Movement and organized thousands of people to plant tens of millions of trees throughout Kenya as an act of environmental restoration (landing Maathai a Nobel Prize). Outdoor experts are innumerable and often don't appear or behave the way mainstream history has dictated. Look harder. Look deeper. Look for when the "truth" lies. Have few Black people been outside, historically, or have we instead been outside and overlooked?

REDEFINING "OUTSIDE"

What do we mean when we say we are in the "wilderness" or "nature"? In modern history, many people define wilderness as a place without human evidence or alteration. But the vast majority of wildernesses defined in this way are areas from which Indigenous people have been removed, by force or disease, along with biodiversity that thrived in their presence. Socially, these notions of wilderness contribute to the nature gap: the research showing that people with marginalized identities are less likely to engage in outdoor recreation. Many marginalized groups, for example, were and are pushed into residences farther away from natural spaces and experience disproportionate restrictions on transportation. These same groups often view even casual natural interactions, such as hiking, to be inaccessible and extreme. To help create an inclusive outdoor community, this fallacy must be corrected. "Outside" must be redefined.

First, we must recognize that the success of wilderness is dependent upon Indigenous land stewardship, including stewardship by Black and African peoples. In fact, in the last twelve thousand years, humans have shaped about four-fifths of Earth's ice-free lands. We must also focus our actions on Indigenous and therefore natural justice and reparation, which, of course, requires dedicated support of Land Back movement efforts. If we uphold the idea that the Great Outside **must** involve people—Indigenous stewards, conservationists, and trail keepers alike— then "outdoor recreation" embraces the stories in *Been Outside*: a child's observations of nature on her walk to school and bike rides in urban settings represents outdoor recreation as much as summiting Mount Kilimanjaro does.

We center Black outdoor experiences outside the Outside that we hear about most often (the Outside many believe to be thoroughly true). Black cultures have outdoor festivities, from cookouts to Caribbean carnivals, with entire genres of music (griot, calypso) intended to be heard and played outside. And generations of Black families have been sustained by a relationship with nature: fishing, agriculture, hunting. But when it comes to outdoor recreation, Black enjoyment tends to be categorized differently, which perpetuates the misconception (believed by Black and non-Black folks alike) that Black, Latine, and Indigenous people aren't Outside, let alone nature enthusiasts or experts. To talk about outdoor experiences openly and honestly, we have to alter the very definition so that it, too, is inclusive. These writers and their stories spark that conversation.

COME WITH US

Consider *Been Outside* an invitation to Sunday dinner. We're serving signature dishes: preparations of our experience, our knowledge, our adventures. They are placed at settings befitting our cultures. There are many seats, and everyone is welcome to join and partake in this banquet that may look unfamiliar but is deeply nourishing.

First, we share "How We Arrived," six pieces of discovery and self-definition. Writers define who they are, using their experiences in nature to guide them. They confront their internalized colonist culture and concepts, work to overcome imposter syndrome, and embrace nuanced complexities as they agree with, defy, and change long-told narratives.

Next, we showcase "All In," five tales describing how first tastes bloom into world-changing passion and Black autonomy in the outdoors. These athletes, scientists, and designers exist, unapologetically, outdoors. In their craft, they ultimately find their niche by enduring the tough love that nature dishes out.

As we connect past and present, we are actively "Walking Ancestral Paths" through diasporic lands, including Africa, the Caribbean, and the US. With these five stories, the writers honor ancestors and their history and build on their traditions, as younger generations innately do.

We round out the collection with "Growing Together," stories of community and growth from Black outdoor enthusiasts. Here, community builders share how they forged paths and constructed safe spaces for new explorers to be vulnerable and audacious. They nod to guides and allies who are helping equity and inclusion become a reality.

Shared "meals" are necessary steps toward unity and justice. We are honored and privileged to share these stories with you. However, we recognize that important voices exist that have not yet been heard. This book is merely one tour in a lifetime of exploration.

EMBRACING STEWARDSHIP AND JUSTICE

Collecting these stories has been an exercise in coming up against (often unquestioned) mainstream standards. In our circles, as surely in yours, we talk about high-level systemic effects that disproportionately show up in Black, low-income, and gender-minority populations, such as higher rates of health issues, mental illness, and heteronomy. But witnessing these effects in concentration is another experience altogether. In the time it took for us to reach out to these writers and for them to draft their stories, many of them contracted COVID, several experienced the deaths of loved ones, and some lost jobs and funding or suffered extreme constraints on income or access from furloughs and travel restrictions; some moved to escape extreme harassment, while others discovered serious chronic health issues in themselves or loved ones.

Contrasting our experiences in predominantly white and affluent spaces, we saw firsthand how these impediments and losses are not felt uniformly, yet the standards and practices for production are unyielding. For the world to become inclusive, many of these harmful rules must be bent, if not broken. The word *deadline*, for example, was used during the Civil War to mean a line defined by a trench around a prison that (mostly Black) war prisoners were not to cross. If they did, even by sticking just a finger over, they were shot dead.

These stories are intended as a reckoning for readers of every background. Remain curious about the origins of language, social practice, and acclaim, and boldly move away from harmful, albeit commonplace, practices.

Due to the climate crisis, this work is infused with a powerful sense of urgency. As we lose, inch by precious inch, the wilderness we have evolved in and called home for millions of years, we must ignite a desperate desire to redefine "Outside"—and who may care for it with revered authority. We must reframe our history; center Black, Indigenous, and Latine values; and embrace the expertise that has long existed outside of Western scientific knowledge, which may come dressed in African American Vernacular English (AAVE) and cornrows, which may come wearing binders or taking breast mints. Perhaps we are not creating a new world but instead are feeling our way back to a precolonized one.

As you read these stories, poems, and observations, you will encounter references to studies, facts, traditional knowledge, and organizations that may be unfamiliar. We have shared resources and citations in the back of the book to help nurture your curiosity.

Reading this book is an act of social and environmental justice. With grace, these stories can stoke meaningful, exploratory conversation for years to come.

HOW WE
ARRIVED

WHY I ENDURE

Dr. Alex Moore

Situated twenty-five miles northwest of Ann Arbor, Michigan, the Edwin
S. George Reserve is a 1,400-acre forested nature reserve maintained by
the University of Michigan for research, education, and conservation.
At the center of the reserve sits a two-story white colonial-era house.
Four large columns evenly spaced along a concrete porch support the
roof, while vinyl siding hugs each of the exterior walls. Having long since
been converted from a home to an open concept classroom and research
facility, the house is surrounded by an expansive, vibrant green lawn
extending in all directions toward a wall of trees that marks the forest
edge. As nearly twenty of us exited the classroom and stood on the lawn,
waiting to divide into groups, fall colors put on a show: patches of green
and brown below, variations of reds, oranges, yellows, and greens above.

We were nearly halfway through the semester and by this point knew
what to expect of our weekend trip to the reserve. All first-year master's
students in the Department of Ecology and Evolutionary Biology were
required to take the graduate-level ecology course, which had a simple
structure: a lecture followed by a demonstration of research methods
and approaches, and then time for students to work in groups on projects
investigating various aspects of forest ecology. With both theoretical and
applied components, the course provided foundational knowledge for

anyone interested in conducting ecological research and served as a critical gateway for a career in ecology and conservation. On this particular October day, however, the function of the course was also to gatekeep.

Four of us—the only melanated students in the course—stood together on the grass just to the side of the porch, awaiting further instruction. We were a small cohort of master's students who were funded by a National Science Foundation program that aimed to support historically marginalized groups and increase diversity in science. While it was only our first semester of the academic year as graduate students, the four of us were already friends.

We had spent the prior summer together in northern Michigan, sleeping in sheet metal cabins, going on hikes, avoiding ticks, and getting to know each other in preparation for our first year as graduate students. Those three mandatory months in the woods were our introduction to the world of research and public speaking, and while the tasks were often arduous (some days I would spend hours in the sun observing the types of bugs found on different kinds of plants or staring into a microscope to count the number of parasites inside snail stomachs) and at times anxiety inducing (public speaking has always made me nervous!), it was comforting to know we were in it together. Our placement in the same group for the course project therefore made sense, but it also felt exclusionary.

We made forgettable conversation until I heard a familiar booming voice carry across the lawn and land at my side. I turned to find the course professor standing next to me, suddenly addressing our small group. His features were at once ordinary and distinctive—white, tall, and on the other side of fifty, with a bullish voice making an unforgettable declaration.

"I don't think you should be in this graduate program. You don't speak up in class and you're not enthusiastic or determined enough. All of the other students have shown that they are serious about being here, and I don't see that from you. That's just what I think, but I suppose we'll have to wait and see."

The black cat leapt from the picnic table and landed nimbly on the rear windshield of my rental car. It was thin but had a regal appearance, like the cat in Théophile Steinlen's vintage poster *Tournée du Chat Noir*, and its black paw pads pressed firmly against the glass as it sat. Green eyes tracked my movement for several moments as I maneuvered in the back-seat of the car, then inevitably lost interest and turned to the surrounding area for more interesting quarry. From the clearing at the larger of two campgrounds at Haleakalā National Park, there was a lot to take in: old-growth tropical trees stretching toward the sky, opulent birds and flowers flaunting every known color, and a Hawaiian sunset along the mountain range horizon.

I had arrived in Maui that morning, picked up my rental car, and taken the scenic route toward Haleakalā. It was the first vacation I had ever taken, and I felt it changing my life. In the lower-middle-class household where I grew up, which provided for a rotating cast of at least six peo-ple and three animals at any given time, there was never enough money remaining after mouths were fed and bills were paid to have fun. In my family, a "vacation" was an annual road trip from Michigan to Alabama in a bright red Ford conversion van during the heat of the summer to visit extended relatives who didn't have central air conditioning. While these trips were often enjoyable, they also felt like our collective peak. It was as far as we would ever be able to go without more time or money.

As an undergraduate student, I worked two part-time jobs at min-imum wage before heading to graduate school, where I moved up an economic bracket, still made less than $30,000 annually, and could only afford to visit home once a year. During one of these holiday trips, sitting at the small kitchen table in my aunt and uncle's Detroit home, I saw the email appear in my inbox: "Philadelphia to Hawaii, $250." Staring at the subject line and trying to quickly do the mental math (a flight from Boston, where I lived at the time, to Philadelphia was $100), I saw my chance to write a new narrative for myself.

I took it.

From Kahului Airport, the direct route to Haleakalā National Park covers roughly thirty miles on an inland highway surrounded by a flat, grassy expanse that steadily becomes mountainous near the park entrance. The alternate route, known as the Road to Hana, covers almost twice the distance, slowly and deliberately winding through lush rainforest toward Maui's eastern end. Google Maps predicted that the drive would take just over two and a half hours, and I was in no rush. I pulled over at every opportunity. Around each bend in the road, a scene came into view that shook me to my core. Twin waterfalls plunged over a cliff's edge into a deep pool below, and my chest tightened. The rainforest opened into a staggering view of the Pacific Ocean crashing onto a beach in the distance, and tears welled up in my eyes. Rain droplets splashed and ricocheted off the leaves above while a symphony of birdsong echoed in all directions, and I let out a small unintentional laugh that said, "I can't believe this." It was a laugh that conveyed a sense of total shock, as I was feeling something I'd never felt before: overwhelming happiness.

I held onto that moment—that **feeling**—for the rest of the drive, until I arrived at the campground in the late afternoon. Typically, I would have immediately moved on to planning the next thing: making dinner, figuring out how to sleep in a car, plotting a schedule for the following day, but something in me had changed that day and I needed to commemorate it. After a few moments maneuvering around the backseat, I found my journal—a small black leather-bound notebook with an oak tree engraved on the cover and a bright yellow elastic band securing it closed. The black cat wandered off as I slammed the door shut and took a seat at the picnic table to write an entry.

> March 6, 2018. This trip is the best thing I've ever done for myself. I feel it refilling me. I'm doing whatever I want in any given moment. I'm finding myself, learning who I am and where my boundaries are, and existing selfishly. I love this and want to remember it forever.

"It came up in conversation earlier, and we think you should apply for the position if you're interested."

I was caught off guard by the suggestion while sitting at my desk in the American Museum of Natural History in New York City. My mentor awaited my reply as she stood near the entryway to my cubicle, which was separated from the rest of the office by two room dividers and a row of largely empty bookcases. She had just returned from her morning check-in meeting; the "we" in her statement referred to her boss, the director of the small department in which we worked, and her direct supervisor, an established and acclaimed senior scientist and conservation practitioner. My mentor was one of several full-time staff members in the department with supervising privileges. I sat at the very bottom of this hierarchical structure, a postdoctoral fellow.

I was two months into my fellowship, and the museum was soliciting applications for a full-time research scientist position with benefits, paid leave, and a salary bump. It was the kind of "real" job I'd always wanted, though in a city I had told myself just two months prior that I only had to tolerate temporarily. The stipend for my current position would last for only one year, and while I was already applying for other funding opportunities, it would be a nice change of pace to establish roots somewhere, even if that somewhere was New York City.

"I'll give it some thought," I said.

A week later, while taking the train from Grand Central Station to New Haven, Connecticut, I worked on the application materials: a cover letter, my curriculum vitae, and responses to the two questions included in the application. My partner was taking a bus down from Boston, where she lived, and we planned to meet in the middle for a date night touring the campus of my doctoral alma mater and eating the best pizza the East Coast had to offer. When the train pulled into the station at the end of the two-hour journey, I clicked "send" to submit my application. Then I forgot about it for the rest of the weekend.

The following Monday morning, I settled comfortably into my chair, pulled up to my desk, and opened my email to find a message from the department director with the subject "Research Scientist Position."

> Hi Alex, I'm excited to hear that you're interested in the position and wanted to chat about your application. While the letter you wrote was enough to get you considered, I can tell it was written quickly and could be strengthened. Since you have not yet officially submitted, we actually have an opportunity to give you comments on it, and have you submit a new version of your materials through the "official channels" next week.

The suggestion gave me pause, and I sat in a deep sense of discomfort for several moments. I understood what was being offered: nepotism, coaching, preparation for an internal hire. Having never been on the receiving end of these actions before, I didn't know how to process it. I was conflicted, confused, uncomfortable, and a little ashamed. I sat in my uncertainty for quite some time until I finally made a decision: to ask my dad, who often sees more of the picture than the small part I'm focusing on, what I should do.

"This is how it has always worked for everyone else," he said. "Now make it work for you."

After incorporating the suggestions and feedback I received, I officially submitted my application and, two weeks later, received an invitation to interview. The format was straightforward: I would have several one-on-one meetings with department staff, followed by a panel-style interview with the core hiring committee, which included the department director, a senior scientist, and an external member from a separate institution. I had strong interviewing skills and felt good after each meeting. Following the interview session with the hiring committee, the director walked me out of the room and overflowed with praise.

"You did a great job! I could tell that you had really thought through all of your responses, and everyone was left very impressed. We still have a few more interviews to wrap up, but we'll plan to be in touch soon. You should be very proud of yourself." I returned to my office, filled with excitement. I was about to have a real job, I was about to make real money, I was about to have a stable life for the very first time.

A week went by in silence. Then two. On Friday of the second week, I received a brief update via email explaining that the museum was having internal discussions about the funding associated with the position and that the hiring committee hoped to get back to candidates in a couple weeks. Another week went by. Silence. Four weeks after the interview, I had a scheduled meeting with my mentor and the department director to discuss work unrelated to the position. As the meeting came to a close, the director indicated that we should "address the elephant in the room—the research scientist position." Thinking back now, it's difficult to remember the full conversation, but she made her final point very clearly: "We've decided to offer the position to another candidate.

We think it would be best for you to remain a postdoc and then consider applying for a position like this again in the future."

I knew how to read between the lines: We would prefer to keep you at the bottom but thank you for improving the diversity and quality of our applicant pool.

The Instagram story featured four posts, one after another, representing a summary of my trip to Malaysia. The first post had a vibrant background transitioning from orange to yellow across the diagonal with bold white text in the center that read "Places in Malaysia that I don't fit. . . ." Each successive post had a one-word title at the top in the same bold white text ("Chairs," "Cars," "Airplanes") along with an accompanying photo: my bare legs squished into a hotel lobby chair, my bare legs squished into the backseat of a car, my bare legs squished into an airplane seat. It was my first time in Malaysia, and I found out very quickly that with my five-foot-nine frame, I was comically larger than everyone around me.

I had just arrived at my hotel in Kota Kinabalu, Borneo, after a brief but glamorous forty-eight hours in Kuala Lumpur. After navigating the public transit system, shopping at Central Market, and exploring the Kuala Lumpur City Centre Park, I had had my fill of the bustling metropolis and was ready for Borneo's slower pace. My itinerary for the day was simple: rest. The next day, I met with my research collaborator from the University of Malaysia and her colleague—both in ornately patterned hijabs, brightly colored blouses, and jeans—and was given a no-holds-barred guided tour of Borneo.

"The oil palm plantations stretch on for miles and miles here. We know that it's bad for the environment, but it's difficult to make enough money in other ways." I sat in the backseat of a small blue sedan, with both windows open and cool air, heavy with sea salt, flowing through in all directions. Through either window all I could see, planted in evenly spaced rows expanding endlessly toward the horizon, was oil palm trees. Originally introduced in the late 1800s as an ornamental plant, oil palm is now a significant commodity crop in Malaysia after production boomed in the mid-1900s due to palm oil's commercial value.

The extensive oil palm forest, full of bounty and devoid of nature, would seemingly have continued on forever if not for the sharp turn in the road that brought us to our destination: the Klias Forest Reserve. A small dirt road took us from the main thoroughfare to a series of brown buildings on stilts with seafoam-green tin roofs, connected to one another by a raised wooden boardwalk. Upon arrival, we met staff members who gave us a brief presentation about the reserve and then led us on a walking tour of the surrounding natural ecosystems.

The boardwalk cut a direct but unobtrusive pathway through the native peat swamp forest. Birdsong echoed in the interlacing branches above, and nebulous shapes moved through the murky water below, illustrating an ecosystem brimming with life. It was hot, and I was dressed for New York City instead of Malaysia—a black short-sleeved shirt, black knee-length shorts, black socks, and black shoes. Sweat beaded down my forehead, and every few moments I heard the high-pitched whirring of a mosquito as it attempted to land on my face to take a blood meal. I was physically uncomfortable, self-conscious because of my height, and a little bit scared (Borneo is home to many large carnivores and venomous snakes). Despite all of this, my overriding sense was that of contentment.

In the months leading up to this moment, I hadn't felt much. Between managing the betrayal at work and the uncertainty of where my next paycheck would come from when my contract ended, I had reached my limit. I wasn't able to confront those feelings and still take care of my daily responsibilities, so I decided to pack my emotions away for the time being. Then, what began as a temporary solution became an indefinite one. Even when I was notified that I had received a National Science Foundation award that would fund an additional two years in my fellowship at the museum, I didn't feel a thing.

Standing on the boardwalk in the middle of a protected forest in rural Borneo, chatting with individuals who loved their land but also struggled to make a living on it, I remembered that this place and these people were why I had endured to do the work that I do. More than anything, I want to be in community with those who share my values, and I want to support them in their work and in their ability to live their lives fully. And so, in that moment, despite the heat and the mosquitoes and the imprint of the Michigan professor and the museum job situation and everything else, I felt a calming reassurance that I was doing what I was meant to do and becoming who I was meant to be.

TRAGEDY BEFORE TRIUMPH

Dr. A. Bashir

I come as one, but I stand as ten thousand.
—Maya Angelou

On this snowy winter's day, sitting in the living room of my parents' home in small-town Nova Scotia, I'm reminded of the cathartic and meditative role writing in nature has often played throughout my lifetime. As I write, I am often entranced by the natural world around me. At the moment, the lake my parents' home sits upon is completely still, the sky above almost perfectly clear, its mirror image reflecting in the water. On this particular day, I find myself nodding with a sudden realization: writing saved me.

While in pursuit of my PhD in neuroscience, years ago, writing in nature became my life's release valve. When someone at work had done something particularly annoying, inconveniencing, or downright hurtful, I found solace in venturing into nearby Pacific Spirit Park after work, comforted by the smell of pine leaves and the shade of tall evergreens as I sat on my favorite tree stump and wrote my poems. I was also drawn to a seldom-frequented corner of my work building that had a spectacular view of Vancouver's North Shore Mountains. I had many moments of fortuitous clarity while gazing at their perpetually snowcapped peaks. Midway through my PhD, I remember being struck by the realization that a single mountain, as remarkable as it was, almost always paled in comparison to the beauty of an entire mountain range. The power and beauty of the collective was clear to me then, each mountain adding its own stunning dimension, reminding me how much I, too, could use a mountain range, a community, of my own.

As I looked out at the stunning skyline, stanzas would arrange themselves in my mind. I hurriedly wrote down my thoughts, feelings, and experiences in my phone's notepad. Many of my poems centered on my experiences within the lab. In addition to writing about work and school, I wrote about family and society. I wrote about expectations and self-doubt. And I wrote about love and faith.

My religious identity has long been an important part of who I am. I chose to wear the Islamic headscarf when I was a preteen and have been wearing it ever since. I would be dishonest if I said that wearing the hijab is easy all the time. The hijab is an automatic identifier, signifying to my community that I stand with them—a billion of us—united. This identifier also makes me an easy target, so I am often timid and anxious when world events augment the spotlight on me.

My anxiety was at an all-time high in March of 2019. News quickly made its way to North America about a horrible massacre that had taken place in Christchurch, New Zealand. When I heard the news, it was still Thursday in Vancouver, but the shooting had taken place as members of the community congregated for Friday prayers at a local mosque on the other side of the world. I sat on the edge of my bed in shock as I read the news that evening, feeling the post-traumatic stress of having been witness to multiple instances of bigotry during my short life.

I debated for hours whether going in to work the following day was a smart idea. My heart was heavy, and to be quite frank, I was scared to go outside. It is an undeniable fact that hate fuels hate, with the incidence of crimes based in bigotry going up in alarming ways after an initial hate crime is reported. To date, that is one of the most frightening statistics I have ever heard.

I spoke to my mother about my fears. In the long term, going outside was unavoidable, but leaving the protection of my home to go to work so soon after the incident in Christchurch awoke a debilitating fear within me that I found suffocating. In the same breath, I felt the expectation to go on with my experiments as though nothing had happened, especially because I feared being seen as professionally unreliable. Conceal and continue, I remember telling myself.

Deciding to do things differently this time around, I ended up sending an email to my lab letting them know that I was taking a week off to heal. After more than two decades on Earth, I finally gave myself permission to grieve. I sought comfort in family as I grieved the victims of hate crimes that made the news, and those that did not. Since I had begun my graduate degree, the victims of Charleston, Chapel Hill, Orlando, and Quebec City—among many others—had been on my mind and in my heart.

I thought about venturing into Pacific Spirit Park to process my thoughts, but couldn't. I was afraid of being alone and exposed, and I was subsequently dejected, realizing how much fear I now felt for a space that had previously offered me comfort and clarity. Instead of going to the park, my partner and I took part in a vigil at a nearby mosque the day after Christchurch, to honor all the victims of hate crimes in the recent past. It didn't escape me that police were present everywhere I looked, reminding me that it wasn't just me on high alert.

British Columbians from all over the Lower Mainland crammed into the small open space of the prayer area, sitting on the carpeted ground, united in our grief. We held each other that evening and voiced our respective concerns about being outdoors and in the mosque, recognizing the courage it took to leave our homes that evening. As we emerged from the mosque a few hours later, with the darkness of night engulfing us and the North Shore Mountains at a distance, I made my way home gripping my partner's hand tightly, passing through the city center that buzzed with a Friday night nonchalance that I found painfully disheartening.

On that night, the mountain view did little to calm my vexed spirit.

It's been quite some time
Since I've seen a face that looks like mine
In a city
So diverse
I simply don't see
The representation of me
  Untitled, Fall 2018

A month before the attacks in New Zealand, I had started working on an idea to create the community I was desperately craving. After New Zealand, I officially decided to take the plunge into a world unknown.

Sitting in the secluded area of my workplace once more, following a full day of brain imaging on our lab's microscope, I began writing a manifesto for a podcast I had decided to create. The manifesto—dated February 12, 2019—stated, in part:

It does not escape me that there are many little girls and boys who have never seen a neuroscientist who looks like me. My goal with Her Royal Science is to change that, and to give others the platform and opportunity to share their stories, free from judgment.

Her Royal Science is a tribute to all the queens who have come before me, and for the science royalty yet to come, in my lifetime and beyond.

Bolstered by the feelings of grief that I wanted to turn into something productive, I squeezed in time before and after work to kick-start an initiative that would be a safe online space for us all. In the summer of 2019, I launched my podcast, *Her Royal Science*, as an ode to the minoritized. In academia, I could see how much we were forced to code switch, to leave aspects of ourselves at the door in order to blend in. I didn't like the feeling of having to be something other than myself in order to exist in the space where I was spending nearly all of my time.

Her Royal Science became my love letter to my community, a conversational podcast where we could bring all of ourselves. In addition to talking about work and school, we spoke about family and society. We spoke about expectations and self-doubt. And we spoke about love and faith.

We spoke about us.

A year after the Christchurch attacks, I was living in Edinburgh, working as a postdoctoral researcher. I had completed my PhD toward the end of 2019, packed up most of my belongings, and moved to the UK for the second time in my life.

My experience of working in an entirely homogeneous group meant that I became the spokesperson for my race within my brand-new lab. A week after George Floyd was murdered, my supervisor allocated the last few minutes of our three-hour Zoom meeting to discuss the global response. I remember her addressing me while the larger group was present, saying, "Though I lived in the US for my postdoc, I don't really understand why there's such a huge response to this incident. You can help us understand this situation, since you've probably been stopped by the cops before. Could you tell us what that's like?" I initially blinked in response, then took a deep breath.

"I don't think we need to have experienced something personally to have sympathy for others," I said curtly.

"Of course," she responded, with a tinge of defensiveness. "I just thought you could help us understand the Black experience."

Before I could respond, she announced that we had run out of time for our meeting, and said we would resume our conversation soon. We never did.

While Pacific Spirit Park became a place of refuge whenever I felt deflated or overwhelmed in Vancouver, living on a busy street in Edinburgh meant that in order to escape the walls of our home and trek into the nearby parks, I would have to be in close proximity with countless people at a time when we weren't entirely sure how easy it was to catch COVID-19. As close as the renowned Holyrood Park was to my flat, my cathartic trek would simply have to wait.

A few weeks later, my supervisor announced that she expected us to return to work at the lab. The pandemic was far from over, and I was still grieving the deaths of George Floyd, Breonna Taylor, Ahmaud Arbery, and Elijah McClain. "But we've already lost so much time," my supervisor kept saying to me and my labmate whenever we expressed hesitation about heading back to work in the middle of the pandemic. I felt discouraged from taking time off that summer, especially since I had already taken a month off toward the beginning of the pandemic to care for my partner.

Feeling the powerlessness of my position as a trainee, I made my way to the lab—walking exactly fifty-five minutes each way to avoid taking the bus—to carry out experiments that felt unnecessary and ill timed. Conceal and continue, I reminded myself. During experimental incubation periods, I would seek refuge on the grassy hill across the street from my workplace, taking deep breaths without the incapacitating fear of catching COVID, looking up at the often-blue summer sky as I called my partner to request a writing prompt. "Could you give me a word?" I'd ask. He would kindly humor my request, and I would begin to write, my thoughts punctuated by the sounds of birds chirping nearby.

One afternoon, he responded with the word *breathe*, and I wrote, in part:

> I wish I could hit pause
> and breathe,
> without feeling like taking a breath
> could be a misstep;
>
> I don't think I want this career
> if I am required to constantly live in fear—
> traumatized by having to relive
> my deepest aches.
>
> And most of all,
> I'm tired of having to be this fake.

I assumed I was the only person who felt lost in the academic space. As researchers attempted to return to work that summer of 2020, I felt the expectation to plaster a smile on my face as though nothing was wrong in the world.

I was scrolling through Twitter in the middle of my summer hiatus from the podcast when I came across a tweet about Black in Neuro, an organization being assembled to bring together Black neuroscientists around the world, an initiative that was starting just as the Black Lives Matter movement had caught a new wind in 2020. I remembered how hard it had been to find Black neuroscientists when I first began my graduate degree five years prior, struggling to find a face like mine to look up to.

With Black in Neuro, I didn't have to look that hard anymore.

On the first day of Black in Neuro Week 2020, thousands of faces filled my Twitter feed for "Roll Call," a chance for us to introduce ourselves to the Twitterverse and beyond. For once, I didn't have to try so hard to act like everything was okay, to appear as though my work was unaffected by what was happening around me.

The following year, I was invited to be part of the Black in Neuro Week lineup, hosting and producing a conversation that celebrated our intersectional identities. I had the honor of guiding a conversation between a Black-Indigenous-Latine two-spirit clinical psychology student, a British woman of Jamaican descent completing her PhD in neuroscience, and a legally blind man beginning his medical degree. Black in Neuro gave us space to be ourselves, unapologetically. If you had told me when I first started my PhD that a space like that would exist within the folds of academia, I'm not sure I would have believed you.

Going on to then meet a few Black in Neuro members in person following my return to Canada was a magical experience I won't ever forget. We met on a quaint street in Ottawa, hugging as the sun descended in the August sky. Later that evening, as my partner and I drove to a friend's home for the night, I wrote a three-word self-affirmation that I often repeat to this day—

Be loved,
Beloved.

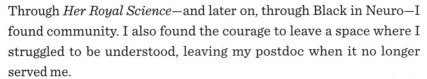

Through *Her Royal Science*—and later on, through Black in Neuro—I found community. I also found the courage to leave a space where I struggled to be understood, leaving my postdoc when it no longer served me.

On this snowy winter's day, sitting in the living room of my parents' home as I write this, I am grateful to be able to reignite my love of writing in nature, entranced by the natural world around me. Transfixed by the lake and the many trees in my view, I'm struck by the same realization I had that one afternoon as I was looking out at the North Shore Mountains years ago. One tree, like a single mountain peak, is beautiful and imposing, reaching heights beyond our comprehension. But a forest of trees possesses an unparalleled majesty, strength, and, importantly, interdependence, using underground mycorrhizal networks to provide support and nourishment preferentially to other trees of their own species. I, too, feel nourished by my network, and I'm reminded of Dr. Maya Angelou's powerful quote, modified from her poem "Our Grandmothers":

I come as one, but I stand as ten thousand.

Though I came into this world as one, with all of you, my extraordinary community, I—quite literally in fact—stand with thousands. For that, I am grateful.

Now, go forth and be loved, beloved.

NATURE, THE PERFECT THERAPIST

Sheridan Alford

As an eighteen-year-old Black woman navigating a predominantly white institution in the Deep South, I had a general understanding of mainstream societal norms. Over time, these standards were shattered or reconstructed in each test, forcing me to prove to myself that I was who I said I was.

My freshman year at the University of Georgia was full of fun, surviving the world on my own and constructing a skeleton of the path I wanted. I had narrowed my passions down to liking animals and caring about the environment, and stumbled on the Warnell School of Forestry and Natural Resources. All my "fun" didn't equip me with the tools I needed to deal with the fall from grace that was my sophomore year. That second year forced me to figure out what Sheridan was made of. That year, I kept a notebook of midnight thoughts that I later transcribed to an app on my phone. Now I can return to them for reflection. In my effort to sort out my thoughts and change my focus to wildlife, I found myself outside more.

When it came to outdoor classes, I enjoyed time in the woods far more than the course material. I found solace in the trees, the birdsong, the gentle movements of nature. During a Bible study retreat to Blue Ridge, Georgia, I would take walks alone and just stand and breathe, an experience that brought forth the realization, I really love this. I love nature. It became my therapist and my friend when I lacked both.

I attribute much of my emotional and personal growth to being outdoors. My family may not have understood what I was going through or why, but they could see that I was at peace outside. Engaging and caring professors offered varied perspectives and created healthy environments that encouraged me to be fluid within my program.

Bird-watching became a constructive activity I could lean on during these ecotherapy sessions. At first it was just a new hobby, but then birding turned into something I could truly grow within. I enjoyed learning about different bird species and anatomy, and I relished the healthy competition between myself and others. The Black birding community was very welcoming, and I made friends with similar goals. When I sought out times of solitude or went hiking with my dog, Zazu, having a safe space to write down thoughts on my phone paired well with being able to use the phone to identify and learn bird species and calls. Nature transformed itself from an escape into a classroom and then ultimately into a healing space.

> Bruh, all this stuff I want to say but can't say because I don't have an outlet. I'm just hostile right now, and angry, and a little hurt about getting rejected from the Arch Society. Could curse everyone out if I wanted, but I'm alone. Can't put it on Twitter because what's the point of that? I need to be studying, but [redacted] that right now. I'll get to it like I get to everything. I need to stop eating so much food and/or work out. Gotta go grocery shopping so I can

stop spending extra money on food that lasts all of 15 minutes. Man [redacted] everything. Turn that frown upside down and get the [redacted] away from me. Finally understand Kanye's tweet rant. [In 2016 notorious music artist Ye West received mixed reactions to a seemingly chaotic thread of tweets on his Twitter account. Some believed this thread was the artist's mental break. When writing this prose, I realized I could identify with the uncontrolled stream of conscious thoughts that Kanye expressed through his tweets.] He wasn't on coke, just a little high strung on life. Yesterday I felt like I was drowning in love that I couldn't express, today I'm flying in a [redacted] jet over the earth because I'd rather be up there than deal with y'all's [redacted] down there. I could cry and run a mile and dance and sleep. Naw, I couldn't sleep, too hype. I still have that graduation poem I wrote him. Probably have to amend it; some things have changed. My head hurts now . . . don't think it's getting enough oxygen. Keep forgetting to breathe.

I'm just naturally nice, I have no reason not to be. Can't tell me you're hungry and then tell me not to get you food if I already made the decision. You get this food even if I'm broke. Mine won't want for something if I can provide it. Overload of everything right now. At least my nails are a cute pink color. Still need a top coat. All these words are clogging up in my throat, like they need to come out but who is here to tell it to? No one, LOL, except Matteo. LOL he's cute. Just goes to show that you can't plan everything because plans change all the time. Just adjust and do what you can. I wonder if we have to recite our Bible verse tomorrow because I definitely did not go over it. SMH, gotta get these priorities back right. Just don't ask me any questions, because I don't have any answers for you.

2/15/16

Reading this journal entry, you may think "peak mental break," but instead it was the storm before the calm. The hill before I reached the valley and figured out that writing down my thoughts helped me cope, when I discovered my outlets and used my resources to express my thoughts in a safe manner. For a person who is always "Cool, Calm, and Collected," a peer-voted superlative award I won three times in high school, the chaotic thoughts swirling in my head felt unfamiliar and disorienting. Like the storm that wipes out the dam, my uncertainty obliterated my ability to effectively express myself. The rushing water then settles into the valley, bringing forth new life, and for me new understanding.

During this period, I was expected to be at my peak, sitting on boards and going to Bible studies, being a social butterfly and going to all the parties. And I was doing all that . . . on the outside, while crumbling on the inside. Every life lesson I still carry today, I learned in that sopho-more-year, ten-square-foot dorm room. Colleges provide some counsel-ing resources, but in the thick of it with classes, organizations, relation-ships, and all the other mentally taxing thoughts, I never felt I had the time to reach out. Get your mental breakdown in and sleep because you have class at 9 a.m. and a test in two days and your boyfriend might break up with you and there's a meeting at 6 p.m.

To cope, I spent my free time outside thinking, struggling to process occurrences before the next one hit. My biggest lesson was learning how to manage my emotions. Time management is a great skill, but knowing when you need to let an emotion go or deal with it later can save you from exhaustion. Walking to class, I made it a point to stand in stillness, not on my phone but just observing. I would notice the American robins that fly to this pole every day instead of worrying about why the girl who just got on the bus would rather stand than sit next to me. I gained the ability to give my brain a break, which allowed me the space to process my thoughts.

> Sometimes I feel like I'm not smart enough to be here. It's my dream school and I'm grateful to be there; truly blessed. I don't know how I got in to be honest and can only thank God. Everyone is so good at singing or drawing, and yea, I can paint, but only decently. I have talents, IDK. Sometimes I'm just like, "dang, why me?" On a lot of things.
>
> **7/22/16**

Ah, our lovely friend. Our friend who tells us we don't belong even though we made it here on our own merit. Our friend who puts a wedge between reality and perception—imposter syndrome.

For years I would say, "I honestly don't know how I got in," with a shrug, knowing that UGA had been my dream school since sixth grade. I took the average number of AP classes accepted students took and gladly joined a multitude of extracurricular clubs. I did all the necessary steps and got accepted early decision—and was still surprised I got in.

Imposter syndrome can come from so many places, many of them social. Feeling like you should not be somewhere because of status, age, race, or qualifications. Feeling like you are not allowed to feel proud of your accomplishments because it's "gloating." These social constraints inhibited me from feeling a sense of belonging. If no one has told you before, let me be the first: celebrate yourself because no one else is obligated to. Hawks don't pass up opportunities for prey because they're afraid other birds will judge them. Animals don't hide their flashiest colors for fear of showboating; they accept the risk of being seen. Reward yourself for your accomplishments, not necessarily through an outward expression, but any way you choose to express love for yourself and all that your life has encompassed. Look back on old assignments and photos and see how far you've **truly** come.

Black is bold
Black is regal
Black is mysterious
Black is serious
Black is classic
Black is an accent
Black is night
Black is all visible light
Black is classy
Black is edgy
Black is Everything
8/17/16

College is where many people learn who they have been and define who they want to become. Having been a social chameleon in high school, hopping between the white and Black friend group and cool with everyone in between, I did not stop and consider whether I was an imposter until someone questioned my Blackness. "Am I the token? Am I not being authentic?" And yet I felt I was being deeply authentic. I was just met with a side I hadn't been questioned about before, thus leading to self-exploration. It was the expression spoken to my face around a group of Black-diaspora students. A comment to add to the mental flurry of a new school, a new environment, and very few people you can ask for justification. The comment, "What are you? . . . Oh, so you're just Black?" Just.

JUST? Oh no, ma'am, no, Pam. I **am** Black. Thank you for asking. I am the many shades of Black that Black comes in, from the black heron to the grackle to the crows and the ravens. The ever molding, shifting, metamorphosing color that can encompass all wavelengths. Being "Black" is everything that you love. There is no "way to be" when expressing Blackness. This realization eventually motivated me to become president of the Black Affairs Council (our Black Student Union), immersing myself in the culture of our Black students and being unapologetically me, because, hun, Black is everything.

The combination of security in my identity while in the predominantly white field of wildlife biology and confidence in my passion led to a healthy confidence in my abilities. People have asked me if I had trouble within my college or felt excluded or judged because I was one of two or three minoritized students. I reply, "No. I felt very secure and people respected what I had to say, **but** I will always fight for those who do have that experience." The imposter syndrome that **all** of us endure is debilitating and sneaks up at the worst moments, but you can learn to fight back with confidence. Create a Done list instead of a To-Do list; write down ten tasks you've completed in the last five days. If you've journaled, go through your old goals and see how far you've come. These moments will never truly disappear, but I assure you that the confidence you have in who you are (not your responsibilities) can expand into confidence you exude in all other aspects of life. Love yourself first.

Yawning at the peak of light
Drying off the morning dew
A fleck of warmth grazing my left cheek
Pause . . .
Is that
WARMTH!?!?!?

That means they're coming
The smelly pads smooshing my face
Colorful clouds pressing down as a shadow looms over from
above
Showers in the middle of the day
And this singsong bird call that just doesn't come around when
it's cold
Time to switch out the winter browns for these feverish greens
Oh how I love to be grass in the spring

2/20/2018

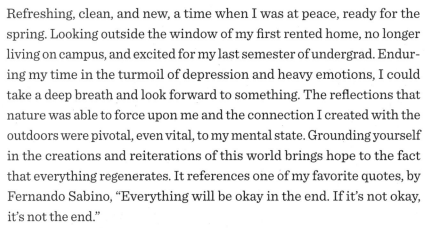

Refreshing, clean, and new, a time when I was at peace, ready for the spring. Looking outside the window of my first rented home, no longer living on campus, and excited for my last semester of undergrad. Enduring my time in the turmoil of depression and heavy emotions, I could take a deep breath and look forward to something. The reflections that nature was able to force upon me and the connection I created with the outdoors were pivotal, even vital, to my mental state. Grounding yourself in the creations and reiterations of this world brings hope to the fact that everything regenerates. It references one of my favorite quotes, by Fernando Sabino, "Everything will be okay in the end. If it's not okay, it's not the end."

The reason I can be so calm now and not overreact to stressful environments is the contentment I've found in letting things be. Nothing can be controlled and everything can be gained. The ants, trees, birds, and wind that coexist so effortlessly and bend with change have saved my mental health and given me vast internal resources. It's not feasible for many to "just go to therapy," so I encourage you to find at least one thing that you can sit in silence and do—whatever brings you peace.

Often confused with happiness and joy, peace is not fun with friends, although that can be an avenue to finding this state of mind. Wherever you can truly be yourself, think comfortably, and feel safe is where your peace lies.

They didn't lie about Summer '16 being one of the greats.
I wish I could go back to 2016.
When I had no focus, only that I liked to go outside.
I had the weight of the world on my shoulders, but a chasm of opportunity under my feet.
There's a solace in having low expectations for yourself.
A hobby is a hobby until it becomes a job. They say you'll never work if you do what you love, but what they don't tell you is that some things should stay a hobby if happiness is to be retained.
People don't tell you about achieving their goals . . . and then being disappointed.
Or reaching milestones that you didn't have before but don't know if you want to reach. Don't get me wrong, I'm forever grateful.
Nature was just more fun when it was just me and nature.

1/20/2021

The age-old qualms of an entrepreneur: doing what you love but reminiscing about when you used to love it freely. I have come to understand that this perspective, often misconstrued as being ungrateful or selfish, comes from the consumers of your work, who do not want you to take a break. I was thrown into my wildest dreams, but once the smoke died down, was it what I wanted? Sometimes fate decides, and my Aries personality bucks against that lack of control.

The internal conflict I must resolve is, How do I create my own lane within the path that was handed to me? I love birding, I love Black people, I love merging the two, but how do I continue to love all these things without becoming burnt out? The answer, I've found, is to shift gears. I reignite my passions by focusing on something new within the realm. It's okay to change your mind or shift course; we are allowed that. I had to remember that true friends and peers are drawn to me for my personality or wisdom or strengths and will be there regardless of my decisions.

In those tenuous years of college, mental health was always a pillar of my passion for nature, but at some point it became my priority. Nature can be the perfect tool in your therapy toolbox. Engage your body as you meander along a trail or rest on the back porch. Inhale the scents of grass and moist earth. Listen to the sound of chipmunks rustling through the leaf litter and eastern towhees searching for fallen seed. Use these metronomes of the earth to keep the beat of your thoughts as you process a difficult emotion. If you reach a wall, refocus on those metronomes and allow the outdoors to carry you through.

One of my favorite tactics is to find a solitary location outside with a pen and paper or notebook. Take one minute to sit and observe, then begin to write or draw whatever comes to mind. The point is to get whatever is bottled up, outside of your head. It can be a rant about the gas prices, something you've been holding onto for months, how much you love your dog, a drawing, or a reaction to your observations. Decluttering your mind at **any** moment may help free up room for the thoughts that need more time.

The poems I've shared are a reflection of mental growth through my experiences in nature. Bending under the weight of my inability to cope, I tried different methods and found the best practices that helped me. Finding an outlet that worked for me was key, understanding that not all methods work for the majority. I reflected on my favorite phenomenon about nature, its ability to persist, and remembered that I am part of that natural effect. Rain, sleet, or snow, the wildlife must live on, food must be found, offspring raised, ecosystems continued. There may be losses along the way, trauma that must be released, habits that must die, but progress **must and will** be made. You got this!

DISCOVERING SEASONAL LEE

Leandra Taylor

Nature is my favorite place to explore, to frolic, to cry, to learn, to grow—the list is as endless as my curiosity. I never imagined myself forging a career pathway in the outdoors, but I've done that and more. Nature has given me endless backdrops to cultivate a deeper connection with and acknowledgment of what makes me, me.

THE ENVIRONMENTAL SCIENTIST

My love for nature transformed into a career driven by my passion to help Black and brown people reconnect with and find their joy in nature. Humans often think of themselves as separate from nature, when in reality we're all part of the same global ecosystem. A few years out of college, I discovered my passion for environmental education and communicating science to the public. To say that my journey into the conservation field has been nonlinear would be an understatement. I stumbled into environmental science as a major after coming in undecided and taking a random assortment of classes that I thought could be interesting. I landed on environmental science after learning more about the impacts of humans on the planet's flora and fauna, water quality, climate. The farther I got into my studies, the more I knew I wanted to be part of the solution.

After graduating with a degree in environmental science, I was immediately humbled by the challenge of finding an entry-level job that matched my interests and skill set. After months of searching, I decided to go the route of an internship to gain more professional experience and further my career prospects. I took an internship with the US Fish and Wildlife Service in Albuquerque, New Mexico, working as a data management intern.

I spent my first two years in Albuquerque organizing and compiling more than sixty years' worth of whooping crane migration data. The data was collected via an aerial survey of their winter habitat at Aransas National Wildlife Refuge in Texas. This was my first taste of the impact of intentional conservation efforts to protect an endangered species and allow for population recovery. I studied the data and watched the population of a critically endangered bird with fewer than twenty remaining in the wild soar to more than three hundred birds.

My move to Albuquerque was my introduction to the world of birds in multiple ways. In addition to my work as a data intern, I also spent time volunteering and bird banding with a local group of ornithologists at Valle de Oro National Wildlife Refuge, being up close and personal with many different bird species, including woodpeckers, sparrows, finches, and warblers. The first time I held and released a bird, I was surprised by how light and fragile it felt in my hand. It's a delicate process to safely extract birds from their nests and place a tiny metal bracelet on their legs. Before the end of the first season, my dad gave me my first pair of binoculars, and I felt like a true bird nerd. I enjoyed learning about seasonal migration patterns, molting, and plumage, and identifying birds by their flight patterns and songs. Bird-watching quickly became one of my favorite ways to connect with nature. I still indulge in bird-watching and nature journaling everywhere I go.

My experience with geographic information systems was my foot in the door; my adaptability and hard work paved the way. After completing my internship, I chose to refocus my career path on opportunities that included more outreach, education, and community building. My niche in the environmental field is in partnership and relationship building to foster community connections with nature and outdoor spaces.

THE MOUNTAINEER

For most of my life, I've had the luxury of living in cities in or near gorgeous mountain ranges: Colorado Springs in the Rocky Mountains, Albuquerque and its Sandia Mountains, and most recently Asheville, North Carolina, in the Blue Ridge Mountains. Despite living so close to the mountains when I was growing up in Colorado Springs, I didn't start to explore my interest in hiking until I lived in Albuquerque. I joined Outdoor Afro as a volunteer leader in 2017 and found an entire community of Black people who love nature as much as I do. It was mind-blowing and affirming all at the same time.

In 2018, I joined a team of all-Black Americans and volunteer Outdoor Afro leaders from across the United States on a journey to climb Mount Kilimanjaro in Tanzania, Africa. I was the youngest and least experienced hiker; this trip was a lot of firsts for me. My first time camping and backpacking. My first time menstruating during a multiday backpacking trip. And, most important, my first time taking a poo in the great outdoors. Despite all of the things I was telling myself I needed to know to prepare for this climb, I knew I was going to do it. We trained for a year in our respective home states before convening in Arusha, Tanzania. Each day of our climb challenged me in different ways, forcing me to confront my personal limitations and fears.

The hardest day for me was day three. Our goal was to start at around 13,000 feet in elevation, climb to 15,000 feet, and end the day close to 13,000 feet to allow our bodies time to acclimate to the 2,000-foot gain in elevation. After lunchtime, we made it to the Lava Tower, a huge volcanic rock that stands almost 300 feet tall. My body was starting to fatigue from sun exposure as we began our descent down the valley that led to camp. My fear of heights quickly came to the surface as we slowly made our way down the trail. One of the guides instructed me to take his hand and lean on him for support as we continued. I reminded myself how strong I was: "I am strong, my body is strong, my legs are strong." I repeated that mantra all the way to camp before collapsing in my tent and vomiting. Joining the team for dinner, I got the most sage advice of my life. Our trip leader, Julius, looked me directly in my eyes and said, "You need to eat, drink water, stop thinking, and go to sleep." I did exactly as I was told and nourished my body before crawling back into my tent and falling into a deep sleep. The next morning, I felt fully transformed, energized, and ready to continue my climb. I hold that day close to my heart as a testament to my strength and determination.

We continued our climb and made our push for the summit at midnight on the sixth day of the expedition. The sky was pitch black and the wind was blowing wildly as we made our way up the glacier ice. Five of us, including me, made it to the peak of Mount Kilimanjaro. I'll never forget how serene and quiet it was at the top of the mountain. We stared at the vast landscape, in awe of the volcanoes in the distance and the glacier ice that covered the peak. Reaching the highest point in Africa was a feeling I'll never forget, but more than anything else I knew that I had reached the peak because I had pushed through my personal limits on day three. If you ask me, I summited Mount Kilimanjaro on the third day. Everything after that was a bonus.

On the mountain, I learned valuable lessons about celebrating myself and my body, embracing and asking for support, and leaning into uncomfortable growth. The most important lesson I learned was that the summit isn't always the top of the mountain. The journey is just as important as the destination. The joy I experienced on the expedition came from celebrating with my teammates and our team of porters and guides.

Mount Kilimanjaro offered one of the most diverse landscapes I've ever explored. That expedition solidified my love for mountaineering. To me, mountaineering is about connecting with others and the mountain itself. I often get lost in the little details on the trail—the pretty rocks, the tiny snails, the strange mushrooms growing in the leaf litter. While the view from the top is rewarding, half the prize is enjoying what the landscape has to offer; no two days on the trail are identical.

THE ARTIST

As an artist, I find endless inspiration in nature, from the colors and shapes, the unique patterns and sounds. My fascination with nature started at an early age; I spent countless hours watching every nature and wildlife documentary on Animal Planet. I still have binders full of crayon drawings of birds, ants and their anthills, butterflies, and many other critters.

As a self-taught artist, I've always struggled with embracing my artistic talent, often minimizing my creativity as just doodles on a page. When I decided not to major in art in college, it weirdly felt like an admission that I didn't believe I truly was an artist. It wasn't until after climbing Mount Kilimanjaro almost a decade later and confronting personal limitations that I realized how far I had strayed from my childhood dreams. In the months leading up to my expedition, I leaned heavily into art as another language to tell stories and express emotions that I didn't have the words to articulate. I began to explore different media: colored pencils, watercolor, acrylic paint, oil paint, and gauche.

A collaboration between Outdoor Afro and Eagles Nest Outfitters was one of the first tangible opportunities to celebrate my creativity while designing a pattern that told the story of our epic adventure. I drew inspiration from the expedition to Mount Kilimanjaro and the time we spent in Arusha. One of my favorite parts of our trip was when we ventured into the local market to get our hair braided before our climb. The market was saturated in vibrant colors and energy, encompassing fruit stands, shiny trinkets, and gorgeous African prints and fabrics. We spent time shopping at different vendors, buying gifts, fabric, and tailored clothing. Throughout the trip, I was in awe of the vegetation and colorful flowers that covered the lush landscape. I wanted this pattern to embody elements of our trek and the mountain itself. I decided to incorporate the topography of the mountain and center the design around Uhuru Peak, the highest point on the mountain. The Kili Mapp Kili DoubleNest Print Hammock is one of my proudest creations. This hammock is a celebration of my Black joy in nature. It brings me so much happiness to see people enjoying and relaxing in this hammock.

I have had the pleasure of designing multiple products with Outdoor Afro and brands including Smartwool and KEEN. The projects have encouraged me to dream bigger about the places my art can take me. I am an artist; I always have been. My journey as an artist has come full circle. I've been intentional about nurturing my inner artist and exploring different forms of art: painting, drawing, sculpting, and embroidery. I always knew I wanted to pursue art but hesitated out of fear of failure. My artistic journey now consists of embracing my inner artist and sharing my work and my story with those it resonates with.

THE COLLECTIVE

I used to feel like I had to decide on a singular path for my life, but the biggest realization of my journey has been that I don't have to choose among the most essential parts of myself. I've found true freedom blending my passions and pursuing the life I've always dreamed of.

The Environmental Scientist, the Mountaineer, and the Artist each represent a milestone and a season of self-discovery. The lessons I've learned in each of these seasons of my journey have allowed me to move with confidence and lean into discomfort with growth in mind. Now I spend my time trying to find new ways to share my love of art, science, and nature. I look forward to continuing to connect with different interests, passions, and people that inspire new perspectives and possibilities.

RETURN TO SENDER

Dakota Lane

At the core of this poem are bittersweet glimmers of grief, along a disrupted, cyclic trail of mourning, and the paths to acceptance (of ourselves, others, the past, future, and reality) we face.

>There has never been any space for me here
>"You can set your things down there" There
>where mold has already made a home Do
>you not have a bed for me or a clean
>floor   board "The green
>mold cabrini will be your pillow," he left, "it does not creep"
>Time stands still
>
>The mold does not—it crawls toward the
>drip,
>drip,
>drip of the showerhead and down the drain and down the
>sewers
>out into the lake

I stare at it sometimes. Creeping in the out pipes.
I walk along the South Shore
for some time
to stand in your kitchen—high waves feed the lawn
"A home cooked meal, fit for . . . for you" she says stirring a pot
But it's water "and I can teach you to make it"
But it's water
The old grandfather clock swinging
chips away and chips and chips and chips:
she makes a homegrown dill dip for hers—she doesn't teach
me to make water
she doesn't make any for me

I step and I stumble,
racing past mirrors over running sinks in public restrooms
that scream rejections
high winds force-feed beach sand to my eyes
crying long tears to substitute goggles
as I stand on the pier, breathe and, 113B,   dive

The water accepts me
mold spores carried in from the waves
form distant pocket galaxies I kick through the ether
seaweed greets me as I kneel on a tombstone with my last
name
and my fingers scour under the lake floor for

someone's touch. I find another hand, an arm
in the silt, we grip each other
their fingers trace my skin

you see flashlights casting shadows of dune grass
above the water line while fish choke
on rusted bullets shells and dogs bark
scaring gulls

red and blue lights fall across my
shoulder blades—mold spores starscream—the
tombstone trembles and the hand squeezes my hand
three times
An earthquake grows tormenting mussels
resting on anchor chains and mold spores scream louder
The hand burns a thumbprint into my skin and violently
retreats

Massive chunks of the sky plunge into the lake
like melting glaciers. Mold spores starscream screeches
with full lungs
in choir with barking dogs. I run a hand over
my brand-blessing. I can't hide
I can't escape

I learn to become water
and disappear.

FLYING FREE: ADVENTURES OF A SCIENCE CYCLIST

Dr. Karine A. Gibbs

Several years ago, as my professional research career was expanding, I was disappearing. Perceived penalties for being myself stymied me. I felt as if I were rowing through an ocean of hidden riptides where every oar stroke might capsize my boat and take me under.

One spring afternoon in front of my laboratory, I no longer recognized the scientist I had become. I scolded a student for not finishing an experiment fast enough and questioned their commitment to our research and their education. As I was speaking, memories hovered at my mind's edge: hearing the same and harsher words from peers. But what halted my tirade was the student's glistening eyes and tilted chin. I abandoned the conversation and later apologized to that student, but on that day, I still seethed inside. I continued to rant internally even as I missed yet another family dinner. My frustration had many targets—the student, myself, our research. In my mind, each was responsible for this alleged research failure.

These emotions ebbed only when I pounded on my bicycle pedals as I raced along the riverbank. By the time I rolled my bicycle home, those memories rested in the front of my mind. I cried that night. In the morning, as I rode my bicycle along that same riverbank, I realized I could not continue to be **that** scientist. Despite potential professional costs, I had to choose to be **myself**, in my science and my activism.

Bicycles can be social catalysts—important for the environment, livable cities, and female freedom. Bicycling can bring communities together. Riding a bicycle teaches independence and responsibility and can serve as an impetus for social change. Indeed, the history of bicycle riding reflects our communities: good, bad, and in between. Bicycles can unite disparate groups over a single cause. Consider Vision Zero, a network whose goal is to halt traffic deaths and injuries, regardless of transit mode. Bicycling can provide an escape from societal constraints. Being on a bicycle can also reflect the challenges of being in a minority. Indeed, riding my bicycle shifts my perspectives and priorities in unexpected and joyful ways.

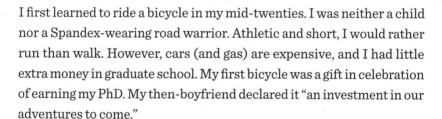

I first learned to ride a bicycle in my mid-twenties. I was neither a child nor a Spandex-wearing road warrior. Athletic and short, I would rather run than walk. However, cars (and gas) are expensive, and I had little extra money in graduate school. My first bicycle was a gift in celebration of earning my PhD. My then-boyfriend declared it "an investment in our adventures to come."

That first bicycle has stayed with me through delights and frustrations as my career, family, and activism have grown. In the past twenty years, we have ridden along the coasts of islands accessed by automobile-restricted ferries. We have enjoyed sunsets over urban rivers on bridges closed to automobiles, with ducks and geese chattering on the water below. Some of my favorite moments were those days in early spring when ducklings along the Charles River waddled behind their parents. At least one usually fell out of line and would start to wander. Bicycling gave me the freedom to be myself and to enjoy small and large moments such as these. It provided a respite that was sometimes hard to find in my professional life.

These days, I ride my bicycle almost every day, navigating an urban environment. Although concrete and steel, asphalt and cement dominate the landscape, nature reclaims the streets. Wild cabbage peeks through the sidewalk cracks. Wild onions sprout from the smallest opening along a sewer line or grate.

Now as I ride, I fly along the streets, unburdening myself, even if for only a few moments. I am free from pressures, expectations, and frustrations . . . free to enjoy and focus on a single time and place. This feeling results from total immersion in a physically and mentally demanding activity. While I am in this "flow state," I am moving while connected with nature around me. It can feel like a divine gift to have moments such as these that allow inner reflection and strengthen resolve.

When I'm on my bicycle, I perceive my surroundings at a slower pace than when I'm driving a car. At this slower pace, I'm likely to stop for groceries on the way home. Or I am tempted by cupcake aromas wafting through the open doors of a local bakery. (Studies show that bicycle lanes increase business profits, partly because people on bicycles are more likely to stop as they roll by.) For example, at one intersection on my way to work, coffee tables line the parklet. Conversations about the latest senior center can flitter through my helmet. Children wave as they walk across the street, hand in hand with adults, on the way to the nearby elementary school. Wispy giggles follow as I ring my bicycle's bell with a small wink.

Such chance encounters happen often. They remind me of the social nature of bicycling. Indeed, photographs from nineteenth-century America through today show this sociality. At the dawn of the women's suffrage movement, people would use bicycles as transport to get to meetings. Cyclists of all races used promenades in parks, which provided a nature-filled resting place in the urban environment. Before the pre-dominance of the automobile in the mid-twentieth century, bicycles pro-vided a way to gather friends and suitors alike. Women achieved some freedoms with the bicycle, befuddling the male-dominated leadership and inspiring newspaper editorials. These social threads remain today. Meetup groups provide spaces for like-minded bicycle enthusiasts, but spontaneous meetings occur too. I enjoy bumping into colleagues as we commute along the bicycle boulevard. We discuss not only scientific ideas but also nonsensical ones. I also appreciate bicycle parades and demonstrations that allow us to unite behind a cause or raise awareness of the inadequacies of the urban street grid.

Over the years, riding my bicycle has continued to energize and empower me. I am invigorated when I bicycle farther than expected or when we try a new adventure and then arrive home safe and tired. I am empowered when I stand up in local public meetings to ask and then demand safer conditions for bicycles and moderate-speed vehicles. Seeing and hearing how others feel powerful from this activity is also inspiring. Bicycles can create opportunities and transform self-images. Organizations teach children how to ride and maintain their bicycles. In the process, their members build confidence and skills.

Bicycles can also improve personal safety as bicycling allows one to travel through an area faster than on foot. On my bicycle, I reduce my commute home to a quarter of the time walking would take. I sweep past silent, eerie corners, especially prominent on short winter days when darkness blankets the commute hours. On my bicycle, I am not invincible, but I am powerful.

———

Yet, riding a bicycle comes with physical as well as other risks. When I ride, there are moments of annoyance and sadness—reminders that we live in an inequitable, and sometimes unkind and unjust, place. I do not shed my womanhood or melanin when on my bicycle. "Hey n——" is hurled from a truck barreling down Beacon Street and swerving into the unprotected bicycle lane—my lane. I'm still not sure if it was the menacingly close vehicle or the words that caused me to drift right (into the car door zone) and slow down (but never stop!). Or perhaps it was the averted stares of the people walking on the sidewalk who heard and saw.

I see this avoidance of uncomfortable truths in some of my colleagues. It occurs when I bring up senior faculty scolding juniors or inappropriate reviewer comments on a paper. I shamefully avoid, too, choosing words carefully and when to share or not. As I age, these experiences wear on me, not to mention my worries for the scientists rising behind me.

I am a Black female scientist and professor. My life and movements occupy a place where some feel I don't belong. I have learned, with the help of bicycling, to practice choosing myself. I have learned to let go of others' unfounded criticisms and slights. I choose to hold on to my self-worth, knowing that I stand on the shoulders of those who came earlier and suffered much worse. I choose to strive to be an effective, critical, and compassionate teacher and mentor. I center my interactions on a simple premise. Each person has the potential to learn and succeed given a supportive environment.

I have heard some peers—scientists across races and ages—say that we can (should?) leave cultural struggles and histories at the door and focus on "the science." Not all scientists, of course, feel this way. But there is a consistent undercurrent endemic in some decision-making rooms and conferences. I see now, more than when I was younger, why it is important for me to show up and be me. I enter these spaces focused on judging the science, not each other, and with an openness to something new. And it's not only me; like-minded scientists abound. Indeed, our experiences "outside the door" shape who we are as we enter and move in the scientific world, and that makes science research richer. Bicycling is a bit similar. With more types of bicycles on the road, there is a greater diversity of people, by age and socioeconomic status, who ride. This rise in ridership encourages others. The diversity of people on cycles pushes towns to improve the road so that we protect the most vulnerable riders: the elderly and children.

On bicycle wheels, I occupy a place, not always welcomed, sometimes tolerated. Although people on bicycles do not impact the time of people driving, bicyclists are often deemed nuisances and unworthy of access to streets. Nonetheless, to every "Get off the road," I choose to respond with a smile and eye contact. I remind them that I am here, and my body has value. I choose to ignore drivers who glare at me and instead smile at the person who waves me forward at a four-way stop sign. As a toddler, my child had the best response: a beatific hand wave and giggle. More than once, I've caught a half smile or chuckle after my child's lighthearted gaze met that of the traffic-stressed adult driving next to us.

Some days when we coast down our urban street, my child will say with eyes closed, "I feel like I'm flying!" Such days bring me back to the 1980s when I first rode, seated on the front handlebars of a friend's bicycle as we raced to her house after school. These moments feel like receiving an expected triumph in a challenging experiment. Imagine glowing bands illuminated on a plastic gel indicating that one's hypothesis was correct. In these moments, I am giddy like on the days that I receive an acceptance letter after months of revising a manuscript. There is a release of expectations, worries, and guilt. I focus on the space ahead and the rhythm of my feet: up, pause, down, pause, up.

On a bicycle it is easy to feel childlike joy. In many cities, bicycle parades are family gatherings where those of any age can join. For example, there are bicycle derbies from the spring through the fall months in the Boston area. At these gatherings, music and the squeals of adults and children sharing skills combine into a soundtrack, and we can relax into a collective, shared experience. In Oakland, California, the "Black Joy on Wheels" annual parade (blackjoyparade.org) embodies community spirit and inclusion. It is a time to reclaim the streets as a space that includes people moving at slow and moderate speeds, to reclaim the city as a space for people of all ages, regardless of cultural or monetary status. It is a gathering that allows riders to feel joy, share laughter, and enjoy mastery of a skill.

Research science shares much with these bicycle parades. We work in teams, using different and complementary skills, to learn more about the natural world. With the right experiment, I can enter the flow state, becoming one with the question at hand. At the end of the day, I am in research science because I love the joy of discovery and intellectual creativity. I love that moment of triumph in an experiment or arc of experiments that nourishes my desire to return and do it all over again. I am here now, no longer fading, in my laboratory and on my bicycle.

ALL IN

THEY'RE JUST ACTIVITIES

Natasha Smith

Before I say that I am anything, I must first declare that I am Black. I am a Black woman, a Black skateboarder, a Black motocross rider . . . the list goes on. I love the distinction. It means that no matter what, I am never plain, and I am always adding to the list. Black surfer is one of my newest titles, and my favorite. I think the universe was saving that one for just the right time.

On my first visit to California, I wanted to experience as much of the place as possible. I took a surfing lesson and had a great time but didn't actually get it. When I got home to Virginia Beach, my dirt bike broke and, to be honest, I wasn't that interested in fixing it. It was hotter than usual that summer, and a lot of my friends weren't riding regularly. The instructor had mentioned Costco had surfboards for $100, so I picked one up. I spent that whole summer at the beach. Several times each week, I packed my surfboard into my car early in the morning and drove out there. The surf community at my first beach was small. By the time I started to figure out surfing, I knew all the other surfers by name. They taught me a lot and encouraged me to try surfing in California. A year and a half later, I found myself sitting in a van on the Pacific coast, surfing more than I was working, and living well. A ninety-minute surf lesson at Pleasure Point had changed my entire life.

When I talk to Black people about surfing, one of their first questions is how I got into such a predominantly white activity. The brief story I just shared always feels too simple. There should have been a beloved teacher or family adventure, but really it was just me with a Groupon on a work trip. When I thought of California, I thought of surfing, so it felt like a natural decision. My race and gender have never affected whether I pursue a new hobby or project. Before my lesson, I never thought about the fact that I would be the only Black person in the water that day. The only thing on my mind was how cold the water might be in April (and I was right to be concerned). I quickly learned the difference between the chilly, peaky waves of the Pacific and the warm, mushy Atlantic I was used to.

Virginia Beach is a really big town that spans from a newer downtown to the touristy oceanfront, then winds down through some pretty countryside that touches North Carolina and all the way up to Norfolk, home of the largest naval base in the world. I grew up near the tourist area, so we dealt with the yearly influx of people from the north and west seeking a coastline. With the community being home to a lot of high-ranking government and military officials, as well as the poor left-over Confederates, misogyny and racial tension swirled through constantly. I was fortunate enough to maintain a childlike naïveté about the effects of race until much later in life. I tended to blame any negative attention on the fact that I was a girl. Now, when people ask if I feel safe as the only Black person at the beach, I almost have to laugh. I grew up racing motocross in the backwoods of the Southern states, so the beaches of California are far from the most challenging racial environment I've ever had to navigate—and I used to do it without a second thought. I've slept in many homes that had Confederate flags stamped with Southern pride hanging in the garage. I just figured we needed a new flag for Southern pride because I knew I couldn't fly that one.

Because of that type of social ineptitude, I never know if I'm qualified to give advice on starting new things. The biggest part of starting a new hobby is simply getting over the anxiety of participating. I know I can't just say don't think about that, but that's what I do. Once my helmet is on or my wetsuit is zipped, I shouldn't be thinking about who's looking, because I have to do a thing. Focusing on bettering myself a little each time attracts positivity from other people. I've also realized that many altercations start because a beginner does not realize they're in the way. I always focus on learning how to stay out of the way first because of moto-cross. If you're not going as fast, stay to the right. Hold a predictable line. If you fall, do your best to get off the track. These are things that keep the more experienced riders from landing on you. Similar rules apply to snow sports and other sports where people of different experience levels share the same course. Learning how to be predictable can help maintain the vibe and make it a little easier for you to figure everything else out. Lessons and camps are my favorite ways to start new things because I'm someone else's responsibility. They'll tell me right from wrong until eventually I'm comfortable navigating it on my own. And there's very little chance I'll get yelled at.

That's not to say that each reaction is not influenced by prejudices. I've seen the same infractions, such as dropping in on someone else's wave, by people of different demographics get different responses in the session. When I find myself in those situations, I try to think of it as lightly as possible. I don't have the energy for hate, so I'll make an empathetic analysis of their actions, telling myself they don't have the coping skills they need, so that I can go back to focusing on whatever I wanted to do that day. Even if there is a bad interaction, I can always find some small victory at the end of each session if I at least participated. If the surf is bigger than I'm comfortable with, I don't even make it a point to ride a set wave. I will take the small victory of having made the paddle out, and if I catch a bigger wave, cool.

Small victories lead to eventual success. I have plenty of sports-related testaments to this statement, but building out my van is a more universal example. I didn't actually know how to build anything before I got my van. A strong base of knowledge in Legos made me the family furniture constructor, but I had no freehand carpentry experience. The first bed in my van was a piece of plywood on Ikea table legs. My dog has only recently become brave enough to sit on its much sturdier replacement while I drive because it used to flip over when I hit the brakes hard. Once again, persistence and focus on the task at hand brought the right people to me—a small victory. One day while I was working on the van in a parking lot, a hardware store employee who was collecting carts taught me how to build a basic box frame and how to brace it. From there, I built it over and over, better each time, until I had the home on wheels that I wrote this piece in. There were many small victories and some defeats, too, and I don't know if any project of mine is ever truly finished, but I'm glad I didn't save up and let a company do it for me. After all those small victories, I gained a wealth of knowledge—and a van. I'm proud of it and everything I do in it, and I can develop and specialize it for any of my new interests.

I hope some of this resonates with someone out there. I hope you can remember to just focus on the task when you start to feel people's eyes on you. I hope you can excuse some weaker-minded person in the moment so that you can maintain your focus. I hope you choose happiness whenever it's available. I will say a million times: if you have ever seen anyone do anything that you thought looked fun, you are just as human as they are and you have every right to try it out too. And if you like it, I hope you share it with someone else who didn't think they could do it either.

AN EVOLVING ADVENTURE

Amber Wendler

I squirmed out of my sleeping bag, leaving its warm grasp for the crisp Vermont air. As I slowly unzipped the tent, trying not to wake anyone, I could see my breath forming small clouds in front of me. My eyes squinted as the bright orange light pouring over the mountains reflected on the pond's surface and the white snow delicately blanketing the ground and surrounding pine trees. Everything seemed so still.

I zipped the tent back up and pulled on my hiking boots, the first pair I ever owned. Just a couple weeks before, I had gotten up early and waited in line outside the REI in Boston to browse discounted gear. I walked out of the store that day with slightly used hiking boots and a daypack for around $50 (approximately five and a half hours' worth of work at the campus call center). My roommate had let me borrow her winter jacket and the university outing club provided all the camping gear.

Here I was on my second camping trip ever, and it was already more intense than the first one just two months before at the beach. As I walked toward the pond, I saw all our food and cookware still scattered on the picnic table from the previous night. Shortly after we struggled to make dinner in the freezing cold, snow had started coming down out of nowhere, or so it seemed at the time. Who knows if I even checked the weather. Many of the students on the trip had just met each other for the first time, but our increasingly numb fingers and exhaustion from a long day easily brought us close together. Without hesitation, all eight of us piled into the one six-person tent that was set up. No one had the energy to set up the second tent or clean up the food and we dozed off in the comfort of each other's warmth as the snow accumulated around us. Thankfully, no bears appeared that night, but after several years of trekking and camping in bear country since then, I now know better than to leave food out overnight.

Trips like this made me determined to go on as many outdoor adventures as possible and lead my own outings, but I had a lot to learn. Many of the other students grew up exploring national parks, felt comfortable starting a campfire, and knew all the outdoor lingo. While my childhood was not void of experiences in nature, it looked a bit different. My parents had spent most of their lives in New York City with limited access to natural spaces. My siblings and I also lived in the city as kids until we moved to the nearby suburbs. We would go to the zoo, botanical garden, and natural history museum; go on walks at local parks; occasionally use friends' kayaks on a nearby lake; and enjoy time with family at the beach or backyard BBQs. But we didn't go on any outdoor adventures that required more than tennis shoes or explore nature outside of the New York City suburbs. And to this day, no one else in my immediate family has gone camping. While they appreciate spending time outdoors, they often think many of the outdoor activities I engage in are "crazy" and love to make jokes about me out in the wilderness with my "Jesus sandals," also known as Chacos.

At some point late in my adolescence, my perception of what it meant to explore the outdoors shifted from walks and casual hikes in suburban parks to bagging peaks in the backcountry. Perhaps all the outdoor media had gotten to me, but I eventually realized that this narrative was toxic, especially for people like me who are severely underrepresented in outdoor recreation. These days, I have a deeper appreciation for the outdoors—the wide variety of natural spaces and the countless ways to explore them—but I didn't arrive at that realization overnight. My relationship with the outdoors has changed a lot over the years; it has served as a place of refuge, solace, work, and discovery—a place I have experienced unimaginable highs and lows.

After that Vermont camping trip, I primarily used the outdoors as an escape. I was going to school in Boston because I thought I wanted to be in a city, but where I really wanted to be most of the time was up in the White Mountains a few hours away. There I could temporarily avoid my problems, whether related to school, work, finances, difficult relationships, or the injustices plaguing the world. Many weekends during college (except freshman year when I was too intimidated to join the outing club), I exerted all my energy hiking to the tops of mountains, often through ice and snow. "Two mountains, two very sore legs, and over ten hours later . . ." read the caption of a photo I had posted during this time. Summits occupied my mind, leaving little room for inevitable stress and anxiety to seep in. The euphoria of reaching a summit after a tough hike always overrode any other emotions; I felt empowered knowing I was capable of accomplishing challenging feats. This sense of accomplishment and connection with nature grounded me when I needed it most.

I was not alone in these pursuits. Sometimes I was joined by complete strangers, other times close friends, all offering support and sharing in the joys of reaching new heights together. The thought of not reaching the summits rarely crossed our minds. I was hooked and tackled more and more challenging adventures—that is, more ways to escape. These endeavors were accessible because of free gear, low-cost transportation, and people willing to share their expertise, for which I am incredibly grateful. Within a couple years, I got certified in wilderness first aid, led numerous hiking and camping trips for students, learned how to rock and ice climb, went back-packing, ran a trail marathon, and even spent some time working as a kayak guide. All of this experience increased my confidence being outdoors.

I put my developing outdoor skills to use in my first job as a field ecology technician, which involved living out of a tent and spending summer days trudging through forests. I measured trees while wearing a head net and kept an eye out for black bears. That was just the beginning. Not long after, I was off to Ecuador hiking in the Andes Mountains at heights of up to 15,000 feet, observing how the plants change with the elevation, and then sloshing down muddy trails in pristine rainforest searching for birds in the dense foliage during the day, and measuring bats lit by the glow of my headlamp at night. With such high biodiversity in the rain-forest, I saw numerous organisms on every walk that I had never seen before and may never see again. Soon after my tropical ecology studies, I was immersed in long days of marine research, observing whales and seabirds from a boat far off the coast of Massachusetts and snorkeling off the coast of Belize with brightly colored parrotfishes among the seagrass beds. There, I'd stay in the cool water until the sun went down and the sandflies came out. None of these experiences was easy, but it was so rewarding to combine my love for the outdoors and science, two things that have greatly shaped the person I am today.

After graduating college, I did research in a place I had been dreaming of going to for many years, the quintessential location for outdoorsy people: Alaska. My job involved long solo hikes alongside rocky cliffs and glaciers. I looked for Arctic terns interspersed among hundreds of gulls, observing their breeding behavior while keeping a safe distance from their eggs to avoid being dive-bombed (when terns hurl themselves and their sharp bills toward your head). I took small float plane rides over jagged mountain ridges covered in patches of snow to access remote islands and monitor salmon populations. One such island, Admiralty Island, has the highest concentration of brown bears in the world and is known as Xootsnoowú (Fortress of the Bears) by the native Tlingit peoples. I bushwhacked through thickets of devil's club (a large plant equipped with spines on its stem and leaves common in the Pacific Northwest) to look for northern goshawks perched among old-growth trees in the Tongass National Forest.

I cannot believe I'm getting paid to go on adventures outside, I kept saying to myself. Even five years before, I would have never thought such opportunities were possible. I didn't even own hiking boots or binoculars or know any wildlife biologists personally—it all happened so fast. I cherished getting to work outdoors, even if it meant getting stabbed occasionally by devil's club. During my excursions, I couldn't help but think about all the people who would also benefit from experiences in nature but don't have access to these opportunities. I take just as much pride in knocking down barriers for other Black and Latine folks to get outdoors as I do in conducting research—if not more.

Before I knew it, I was starting graduate school in Virginia, and it became more difficult to fit in outdoor adventures with my busy schedule keeping me in classrooms and offices most of the time. I so desperately wanted to escape into wilderness, but the best options readily available to me were not the types of adventures I'd become accustomed to. Going for a walk outside around my apartment complex or university campus simply didn't excite me very much. It's not like I hadn't gone on plenty of walks in other ordinary places, but now it was my only way to interact with nature. I had gone from one extreme of engaging in strenuous ascents and bushwhacking through remote forests to the other: walking a paved trail with sparse trees and numerous people. I knew there was still value to such experiences, but I stubbornly wanted my grand escape, or maybe I just craved a deeper connection with nature.

Soon after starting graduate school, I was gifted a Nikon DSLR camera. I brought the camera with me on neighborhood walks, taking photos of common birds like cardinals and robins. I have always loved birds and while they're what I came to graduate school to study, I had never really considered myself a birder. I hadn't kept a list of all the birds I saw over the years, wasn't very good at identifying birds by ear, and owned only a pair of cheap, small binoculars. While I didn't fit the stereotypical image of a birder, I had always been very happy watching birds. Taking photos of birds was new for me though; it forced me to slow down and be more present. I started to find greater excitement in the nature right next to me—the flashy shoulder patches of the red-winged blackbirds glistening in the fields, the mesmerizing murmuration of European starlings, the eastern bluebirds scouting out the nest boxes along the trail, and so much more. It felt as if I were seeing it all for the first time, like when I was a kid. I didn't need to be in a remote location or engage in strenuous activities or have a grand adventure to connect with nature, but could instead casually walk out my door and simply look around. I ended up falling in love with birds even more.

Still, my craving to escape was unrelenting, so by my second year of graduate school I was driving out West to embrace the wide-open spaces and expansive mountain views I missed so much. However, this time I didn't feel the self-imposed pressure I had once felt to reach all the summits. I felt content making it only halfway up a trail or being outside without a to-do list. I could spend more time reflecting and less time trying to escape—a step in the right direction.

Collecting data for my PhD research became my next adventure. I would spend about ten months over the next two years tracking down tiny bright green birds called Puerto Rican todies or San Pedritos, and their nest burrows in the rainforest and dry forest of Puerto Rico, among other tasks. This project was everything I had been working toward; I couldn't be more excited. Things that initially seemed so unfamiliar eventually become second nature. I still hear the *zhip zhip* of the todies, the persistent *coquí coquí* sounds of the frogs, anoles rustling in the leaf litter, and scaly-napped pigeons flapping loudly through the forest canopy. I can see the small silhouettes of semi-slugs on the undersides of palm leaves, shrimp making their way through small streams, mongoose quickly running across the trail, and bananaquit nests hanging from tree branches.

As beautiful and serene as the environment was, I was there to work and unlike my previous field research projects, I was responsible for getting the logistics in order and ensuring everything went smoothly. Although I was proud of what I accomplished, things definitely weren't going as planned. Although colleagues told me this is how most science research goes, I was starting to get worn down from all the unexpected obstacles, which felt more difficult than any summit I had ever climbed.

At some point, I lost my enthusiasm for going outdoors despite having picturesque mountains, forests, and beaches easily within reach. I realized that I needed to separate my outdoor work and recreation, carve out space to nourish both. Not only was nature a place where I typically felt most at peace, but it was also a place I've always craved to know more deeply and help conserve. With a renewed sense of purpose, I pressed onward with my research while also making time outdoors for some relaxing activities unrelated to my research. This time was essential to my well-being and strengthened my enduring bond with nature.

As I spend more time in nature, I learn more and more about myself and the world around me. I gain new skills and grow more confident in my abilities. I meet lifelong friends. I become more present and find greater joy in simple things, like plants growing along a crack in a sidewalk. Now I call myself a birder despite still having to look up common bird calls. My outdoor journey is an evolving adventure, and just as the organisms I study adapt to their changing environments, I do too. I look forward to continuing this adventure with a more balanced perspective and experiencing all the wonders nature has to offer.

A HOME IN CLIMBING

Sidney Woodruff

Through films like *Valley Uprising*, *Free Solo*, and *The Dawn Wall*, rock climbing has seeped into pop culture over the past few years. Despite its growing popularity, I still view it as an obscure sport. When I first heard of someone rock climbing, I got a mental image of a person dangling over the edge of a cliff without a rope. However, after a couple years of living and working in Yosemite National Park as a wildlife park ranger, hiking past climbers setting up ropes for kids, and watching climbing films with my peers, I began unlearning my misconceptions. Rock climbing often involves scaling vertical and overhanging rock faces while tied into a rope, and it's not as obscure as I'd originally imagined. And yet, I still thought, It looks cool, but that sport definitely won't be for me.

In sociology, "othering" refers to the process whereby marginalized individuals or groups are conceptually alienated from the dominant social group, which typically aligns with sociopolitical power. At first, rock climbers were othered from society through their rejection of materialism and their devotion to a challenging sport. Later, outdoor recreation, including rock climbing, was typically depicted in advertisements, social media, and conversations as predominantly white and affluent, so I was the other to them. In my myriad of outdoor communities, such as hiking and skiing, I was often in the minority, if not the sole person with Black and queer identities, so being the other in the predominantly white world of climbing wasn't necessarily a shock to me. However, I wasn't expecting the **layers** of othering I would soon encounter when I picked up the sport.

Growing up in the South, I found the idea of people looking for rocks to climb far-fetched. Where I'm from, much of the land is private. I could not park along the side of a road and go hike aimlessly, as climbers often do while navigating to hidden routes, because of the risk of trespassing and the likelihood that someone would step out and point a shotgun at my face. I heard countless stories about Black people going missing or found dead in the woods. When you grow up not being able to play outside your own property line, your experience and understanding of the outdoors is limited.

Outdoor recreation in the South often consisted of going to the underfunded community park or visiting the historic Civil War battlefield. Even on the nearby Appalachian Trail, the main choices are hiking neglected, polluted trails or learning about whitewashed Civil War history on trail signs at every turn. Neither of those sounds enticing to me. Outdoor recreationists often describe being in nature as therapeutic, healing, and an "escape from reality." What happens when natural leisure immediately reminds me of my othering reality? Could rock climbing be that escape that I so desperately wanted to find?

My first outdoor experiences came when I began studying wildlife sciences in the later years of my undergraduate career. Many of my classmates felt destined to be wildlife biologists and field researchers at an early age from watching Steve Irwin and seeing themselves in him. Though I joined the field late, I was fortunate to be in a wildlife program that valued field labs and hands-on experience, ultimately leveling the playing field for jobs and internships. During my final year of college, I knew I needed to find an internship that would set me apart from others in my field and provide me an opportunity to go and explore. When I saw a posting through a targeted internship program for a herpetological conservation internship at Yosemite National Park, I jumped on it.

During my initial summer there, Alex Honnold would become the first person to free solo El Capitan, ascending with only a chalk bag and a pair of climbing shoes. I felt proud and excited to work in this beautiful place where such a remarkable feat was happening. Distant friends reached out to ask if I saw him do it. (I did not.) Honnold's climb motivated me to learn and read about it. Unsurprisingly, a quick internet search on "rock climbing in Yosemite" returned images of buff, shirtless white men with long, tousled hair and Forrest Gump beards flashing wide, cheesy grins. I thought to myself, You knew it would be this way, Sidney. Despite the lack of representation, I convinced myself to try it in, of all places, Yosemite—the pinnacle of outdoor rock climbing. I researched what basic gear I needed to start. I committed and spent the money to buy a pair of climbing shoes, a harness, and a helmet.

I asked numerous coworkers and friends to spend a day showing me the ropes (pun intended) and finally found a group of white women who invited me to join them for a day of climbing. I was excited and nervous in equal parts, overpacking food and water as if I would never be under a roof again. During the drive, one of them mentioned to the group that she had recently "sent my first 5.11 lead," and I remember everyone else in the car replying with audible oohs and ahhs, so I felt I was in good hands. I was the outsider and newbie of the group, but I figured that because we were all women-identified, this space would be safe and I could let my guard down.

My guard unfortunately went right back up when the topic of visitors to Yosemite came up in conversation. The group began laughing at visitors who come to Yosemite to hike a short paved trail or have a family reunion by the river. "That's not even considered hiking," one said. "They're always playing loud Spanish music, too, and that's disturbing the peace." My repeated attempts to divert the conversation were dismissed, especially as the conversation moved to why there are so few Black visitors to the park. "Black people just don't like hiking." "A lot of them can't afford to come to Yosemite." "Sidney, I think you're the only Black person I've ever seen climbing." Conversations like these reinforce the notion that to be included in these spaces, you need to be the "right" type of outdoors person—white, affluent, skinny, able-bodied—and behave in the "right" way.

Was I shocked to hear these things? *No.* Did it still affect me? *Absolutely.* I was used to being othered, but what happens when your **allies** exclude you? How could they not see how detached they were from actual allyship and inclusion? Maybe I should have read the room when they chuckled and assured me I didn't need a helmet for the type of climbing we were doing—the kind that involved scaling a 100-foot rock wall using one rope. "Never hurts to be too safe!" I said lightheartedly to ease the air. "Well, it's overkill because you wouldn't fall that far." It didn't help that my harness barely fit over my hips and that I got extremely winded after making it halfway up the wall.

I've thought about what would have eased my anxieties during that first climbing experience. Though they would not have been able to help my hips fit into the tight harness, they could have understood that people find climbing at different times of their lives. I wanted them to recognize that being able to climb mountain peaks didn't make them superior to the people who didn't leave their car on their visit to Yosemite. Regardless of my presence, I would hope that they would take the time to reflect on their perspectives on different racial groups in the outdoors and recognize their own ignorance. I vowed to find a space where I would feel welcomed and my appreciation for safety would be valued.

Despite the discomfort of that experience, I had been bitten by the climbing bug. It was exhilarating to be that up close and personal with the rock. Because I had to maintain full coordination of my body and mind, the experience went from adrenaline-inducing to therapeutic. It forced me to push aside any negative thoughts and focus solely on the present. Even if only for a second, I managed to escape from the reality of the ostracizing moment. At the top, I could turn back, take a deep breath, and see the landscape from a new perspective with a sense of pride and accomplishment. Those positive emotions from the vast and expansive view waned as I was lowered back down to the group and returned to unstable footing and narrowed minds.

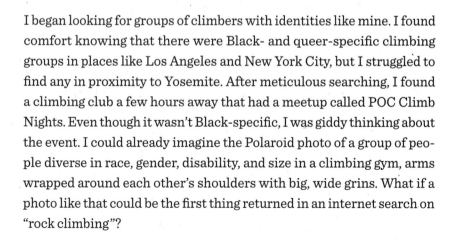

I began looking for groups of climbers with identities like mine. I found comfort knowing that there were Black- and queer-specific climbing groups in places like Los Angeles and New York City, but I struggled to find any in proximity to Yosemite. After meticulous searching, I found a climbing club a few hours away that had a meetup called POC Climb Nights. Even though it wasn't Black-specific, I was giddy thinking about the event. I could already imagine the Polaroid photo of a group of people diverse in race, gender, disability, and size in a climbing gym, arms wrapped around each other's shoulders with big, wide grins. What if a photo like that could be the first thing returned in an internet search on "rock climbing"?

When I arrived at the meetup, held at a climbing gym, I scanned the group and saw light-skinned, white-passing people and one other Black woman, M. We noticed each other and did the mutual Black nod that signaled that we'd stick together the whole night. M was also new to climbing and looking for community. Shortly after the event started, topics of discrimination and racial profiling while climbing came up but were dismissed as rare, outlier stories. When someone mentioned racist and sexist route names, the leaders of the event began listing off routes they had seen, making no effort to censor the slurs. One leader said, "Some people are just too sensitive. Are we supposed to change every route name if one person thinks it's offensive?"

I felt a tightness in my chest and the pressure to speak up, even looking toward M and sensing mutual discomfort. But other climbers were nodding and chuckling at the leader's comment, so I decided to swallow my words with the lump in my throat and stay silent. Why bring attention to myself when all I wanted in that moment was to shrink into the background? I started to question my reality again when no one came to climb with M and me the entire night. Was it us? Were we not good climbers? Despite the isolation, we climbed, laughed, and shared stories about our entries into climbing. M related to my first experience climbing outdoors, and I related to her feelings of being let down by the people who deemed themselves allies. Our patience wore thin when the group migrated to a brewery and a non-Black climber drunkenly put an arm around me, slurring the way through singing along with a rap song playing over the speakers. M and I locked eyes in shock and discomfort as this person said the N-word loudly, swaying to the music, then whispered to me, "I can say that because we're on the same side."

I left the meetup feeling similarly to my other experiences: frustrated and underwhelmed with the climbing community. But I didn't give up. Simple, inaccurate explanations for racial disparities in climbing such as "Black people don't do that" cloak the numerous interlocking structures that exist to prevent Black people from accessing these things and connecting with the Black people who are already doing so in multitudes. I'm often told, "Nature is free. The outdoors don't discriminate." But people in the outdoors do. Aren't these the outsider, outcast, and vagabond type people I keep hearing about? At what point did they forget what being an outsider feels like?

Communities of color are three times less likely than their white counterparts to have immediate access to nature, a disparity often referred to as the nature gap or nature deprivation. The lack of diversity seen in park visitation numbers has been attributed to socioeconomic status, racial discrimination, cultural factors, and environmental degradation. Being immersed in nature offers an escape from harsh reality, with a number of benefits for physical and mental health. But with present inequities, these benefits are distributed unequally across American society by class, race, and gender.

In the same way that we have to push ourselves through a challenging climb, past the first sign of discomfort, we must be able to sit in the discomfort of knowing that there are barriers to climbing and that we may be upholding those barriers in some way. However, the most important next step is figuring out what you're going to do about it. I hope that the climbing community continues to challenge its identity and reflect on who it's keeping in and pushing out. Through my own experiences in climbing, I've tried to redefine what it means to be a climber. I've channeled this energy into exposing those around me to climbing and providing that safe space to try it out, even if it's just once to say they've done it. I've never gotten tired of teaching someone how to step into a harness for the first time, tie a figure-eight knot, and see their ear-to-ear grin as they return to the ground after their first send. Most are shocked that they could do the very thing they said they wouldn't be able to do—reach the top. I know I'm doing something right when people I support in this way follow up with me by saying, "I'm going to get my own harness and climbing shoes now!"

There are the bright sides to climbing too. Groups like Outdoor Afro and Melanin Base Camp are creating spaces where Black people can enjoy the sport in a safe, inclusive, and supportive environment. The climbing community cannot be lumped into one group, so these affinity spaces are crucial and need to be protected. When I'm around other queer Black climbers, I find refuge from constantly being the outsider and gain the innumerable health benefits that being in nature can provide. Those spaces create an environment where it's okay to be a novice, dislike climbing, and be an autonomous individual, not a figurehead or ambassador for the entire Black community. They offer me a place to make mistakes without causing a broad brush to be painted across my entire race. They show us and the world that we are here and we are not outliers. Our reality is that we are Black climbers. Those two identities cannot be separated, nor should they be. We all deserve to have a home in climbing.

OUT HERE

Dr. Shaz Zamore

"Just don't tell me," my mom would say. "I'd rather not know."

"I know you, Ma. Worst case scenario, you're going to be really happy we spoke," I'd reply, same as the last time I headed out here.

"Shaz! Don't talk like that!"

"I'm sorry, Mom. I love you, and it's important you know."

⌒

This story is a love story. And it starts, as many do, in someone else's clothes, on someone else's board, with the guidance of patient friends. Joe, a former snowboarding instructor and a close friend of mine, stood downhill describing balance and how to work the board's four pressure points. Learning with me were my labmates, surfers who were used to boards and balancing. I wanted to learn as fast as them. I wanted to be better than them. I pushed myself harder than I probably should have, enchanted by the promise of a great beyond if only the basics could be learned.

By my third day snowboarding, I could successfully link turns (go from heel-side to toe-side and back again smoothly). Seeing this, my "mentors" took me up to the top of the mountain to "The Wall" and recklessly led me first off a small drop and then off-piste, into pristine, snowy wilds. "We have to get you on powder," they reasoned, claiming that groomed trails, or "groomers," were no place you wanted to spend your time on a mountain.

In the deep snow, I teetered and wobbled behind my friends' smooth and graceful turns. I was unafraid to go fast but unsure of how to do so. I'd finally accelerate only to waddle, flop, or fall. I was consumed with the act of staying aloft. I blew snow away from my face, frustrated and hot as I tried again and again to find balance. There! One long, smooth turn and I started to think I could get the hang of it. I looked up eagerly toward my friends but saw only snow and trees. I called out for them. I called again. Silence. Solitude. My first time on a real mountain, and in a blink I had lost the people who knew how to get me down.

So there I was, stranded in waist-deep powder with no tracks to follow. Other than the trees, there was not a soul in sight. I sat on my board, feeling overwhelmed and increasingly aware of the cooling dampness of my clothes. I hoped someone would come by and give me a nudge, or maybe some hand warmers. Only stillness abounded. Looking downhill, I figured that if I hugged the mountain to the left, I'd wrap around the ridge and eventually end up on a groomed trail. With fervor, I scooted on my snowboard, hands between my splayed legs, which I lifted up if I gained speed. For twenty minutes, I wallowed, waded, and scooted in the snow to no considerable avail. I looked up at my path and saw how little distance I'd traveled. I looked out into the valley, full of ponderosa pines capped with snow, tinged the faintest pink from the sun's low seat in the sky. A sharp twist of fear. I wasn't sure I would make it back before the resort closed. What happens then? Would I be allowed down? Did I just **live here** now? I frantically scanned the vast Tahoe wilderness, feeling utterly small and helpless. And that was it. That was the moment the mountain broke me. I began to weep.

No, *weep* is an understatement. Everything about this moment was childlike, from my snot-covered face to the ragged taper of sobs as I eventually ran out of gas. I at least had found a glamorous place to be lost, alone, and increasingly cold. I realized if anything was going to change, it would be by my doing. I ripped a glove off to wipe some snot off my face. I looked up to the sky, swore loudly, and put my goggles back on.

I wobbled onto my snowboard and strapped my feet back in, shaking and shimmying in a vain attempt to warm up. I repeated: scoot, topple over, dig the nose of my board into the snow. I shoveled the snow off my board. I shimmied again and leaned impossibly (painfully) back so my nose wouldn't dig into the snow. I scooched, teetered, and caught myself; my abs ached. I continued like this, empty yet furiously determined, until a shining moment. A first kiss. One long, smooth, stable glide. My despair was no match for that lilting feeling. I was floating, a particle among snowflakes, fluid and buoyant. Indescribably light, I was free. I would spend years chasing that feeling, that thrilling moment in the wilderness.

I eventually made it back to a groomer. I remember how simple the corduroy felt. I had a new confidence in going fast that also would never fade in the many years of snowboarding to come. Back in control, I felt my anger return and swell. How could my friends have done that to me? Was this some dark joke? It didn't seem like them, but nothing made sense. How dare they! Why would we go out there? Why would they leave me to **die**? I raced down the mountain, furious.

I stormed up to the lodge and flopped down to rip my bindings open. With the sloppy gestures of a petulant child, I grabbed up the snowboard and stomped toward the front door, lost in a mental curse-laden soliloquy for my so-called friends. I stopped dead in my tracks. There was Joe, standing in front of the lodge, holding a cup in two hands, like a delicate bird.

"Hey Shaz," he said gently. "I got you this hot chocolate. We were worried about you; we turned to head back to a groomer and you were gone!" I felt my body soften. He handed me the cup (it was cold—he had been waiting) and wrapped me in a warm, firm hug, the kind that says more than words. When he stepped back, he had a wry grin on his face. He giggled, "Hey, but you made it! What happened?" He took my board as I regaled him with my dramatic saga and how I **actually** snowboarded in powder. Later, in the car, I made a silent promise to myself to never let the mountain break me again. To ensure that this promise was kept, of course, I'd have to return.

That was how it started, my romance with snowboarding. I failed to keep that promise, by the way. The mountain would break me over and over again, often physically. It's taken a twice-broken rib, a torn rotator cuff and a bitter end to a friendship, a bruised ilium, and at least four concussions for me to comprehend that I am minuscule against a mountain's might. I have learned to respect mountains when I play on their broad backs, silly and whimsical.

The thirteen years of unbridled love that followed were hard earned and well worth it. I arced my life toward my most significant other. I moved closer to mountains (eventually to the snowy foothills of the Rockies). I started touring the backcountry, getting dozens of days on snow each season. I even got a husky-Staffordshire mix, a companion who'd love snow as much as I did. In turn, snowboarding brought me to my outdoor home, a place far removed from resorts where I often got constant, unwanted attention.

When I lived in Washington State, riding at a resort meant being stared at, even after years of going to the same place, an obvious local. There is a particular look I received so often that I named it the Unicorn

Stare. Marked by widened eyes and a slack jaw, it is a combination of unabashed surprise and confusion, sometimes with a tinge of disgust. It seemed as though the gawkers had questions that they never asked, perhaps for fear of what I represented to them. When I first noticed being noticed, I'd meet the gaze and hold it until the owner became self-aware and uncomfortable and looked away. This task became too distracting to do every time I went inside to buy a protein bar or grab a drink at the water fountain. These days, I don't look. I keep my eyes focused on where I'm going or who I'm with. I'd rather not know what people think of me.

Where lodges and bars brought Unicorn Stares, terrain parks brought unsolicited Bro Bumps. Shortly after I discovered the thrill of being airborne, I'd frequently join the cluster of skiiers and snowboarders at the top of the park, and wait my turn to get skybound off some jumps. Music blasting in my earbuds, I'd mentally mime the trick I wanted to work on, and get in the zone—when a fist was thrust into view. "Sup bro," some white teenager would say with anxious punctuation. The first time it happened, I was startled, so sharply pulled from my focus. Then I felt excitement—I'm a performer, I love attention, and being deemed cool on the mountain was the ultimate merit. It took a beat for me to realize fully what was happening. My existence—my skin—was being used for clout. Mind you, no one would chat me up on the lift or at the bottom of the park but only at the top, where everyone could see. This person had no desire to meet **me**, Shaz, the ambitious snowboarder; this person was fronting. More eyes fell on me. I was stripped of anonymity and autonomy. Whatever I did in the park didn't represent my learning curve but unfairly measured the belonging of Black people on the mountain. Eventually, my formula became: ignore the weird flex, speed through the park, intentionally avoid every feature. I am a whole human, not a representation of Every Black Boarder Ever, and definitely not One Here to Make You Fly by Association. So to get my airtime jollies, I sought out natural features—cliffs, boulder fields, and fallen trees. I moved away and out, into less-and-less-maintained wilderness.

I'd moved to Washington to get my doctorate in neuroscience. As the pressure mounted and insolence from peers and advisors grew on campus, the Yamakiasham Yaina mountains (the unceded name of the "Cascades") became my respite. Early on, I happened upon a ragtag group of delightful misfits: engineers, programmers, and high-performance athletes who were silly and kind. My new group pushed me beyond what I felt comfortable doing. In those early years, I didn't ride with them much—I was far too intimidated.

Off the slope, they took me to snow sport movie premieres around Seattle. I remember watching professional riders shooting through the air and *pap-pap-papping* down a pillowy run, and thinking, "I want to do **that**." I had a new mission. Slowly, the laid-back styles of my other riding buddies ceased to satisfy. I wanted more, bigger— impossible.

We started to ride sidecountry (high mountain terrain accessed from lifts), then slack country (hikes out of bounds from resort summits). We'd dip in and out of avalanche territory, everyone equipped except me. To get the necessary avalanche training and all the avalanche gear, including a board that splits into skis for easy ascents, would cost around $2,500—a feat on a graduate student salary. It took me a year of peanut butter and jelly sandwiches and dumpster diving to save up for gear: a plastic shovel, a five-year-old beacon, and a secondhand, shop-made splitboard. The probe was the only device I could afford new. Desperately infatuated, I scraped to get my AIARE 1 (American Institute of Avalanche Research) certification. I used someone else's avalanche gear, a solid board, and rented snowshoes. A friend dropped me off, and

I finessed my way into a little-known co-op at the resort. That sacrifice invited in ten years of advanced and expert riding.

I've since upgraded my academic status and income and thus my gear, but I hung on to that original snowboard and beacon to open the door for other beginners like me. My certification lapsed, as the renewal class now costs twice the price of the level 1 certification course. Instead, I'd attend conferences and talks and consume far too much educational content online. Most important, I continually talk with my teammates when I'm out here in these avalanche-prone wilds.

We're always talking. Primarily about conditions—avalanche forecasts, what the snow looks and feels like, changing weather, how we're feeling in our bodies—but once we have a few runs under our belt and the snow feels stable, the conversation can wander to other things. There's no such thing as "normal" in the backcountry. Every single person is flippin **weird**. It was easy to open up to these white middle-class men I shared a bizarrely easy kinship with.

On a hike back from a sidecountry run, I was chatting with Michael, a member of the crew, and mentioned a time someone completely disregarded my knowledge in the backcountry. I had brought a friend, a man, out to Kulshan, and we were stopped by another rider who wanted recommendations on where to go. He approached and spoke directly to my friend, standing a few feet away. "Oh, I'm new here, too, you'd have to talk to Shaz, they know this place way better than I do." I smiled gently and asked what kind of riding he was hoping to do. He paused and made a face briefly, then turned to my friend and answered my question. My friend replied again that he didn't know. I volunteered a few areas, fun but stable. He looked in the direction I pointed with visible stiffness, quite clearly not trusting what I was saying. Why would he? A Black person on the mountain is uncommon, in the backcountry is rare, and with androgynous expression among the rarest of all. I'm used to people struggling to process me, but by this point, I'd long given up on trying to convince doubters of my expertise. "It's up to you," I shrugged, "but I really wouldn't be out there alone if you don't know where you're going. Safest way out is that way." I pointed, and indicated to my friend that it was time to go.

Michael listened intently. He was an unabashed conservative and an impressive, well-rounded athlete. "I don't believe that!" He exclaimed. "That's just insane! People tell me that Black people don't snowboard, and I tell them I ride with a Black person, **and** they're queer, and they **rip**!" I laughed. That was generous. I've seen Michael bust out a text-book rodeo (backflipping over your shoulder) for the very first time in the backcountry. I'm not nearly as good.

We were practiced at trusting each other's word—our lives depended on it! Opening up about tough experiences was invaluable, especially in Seattle, where privileged people loved to assert that our marginalizing experience wasn't, in fact, marginalization. Out here, in the backcountry, no topic is off-limits.

Bonded, we went beyond, to bigger, higher, and deeper terrain. Scarier terrain. Call-your-mom-before-you-lose-service terrain. Years later, we'd meet at a premiere, this time naming ranges, specific mountains, and even runs and famous cliffs that we saw in the films, some of them notched on our belts. With great fortune, I have never been buried in a slide, largely because my love and trust for that first backcountry group—many of whom I still travel to ride with today—kept me humble and aware. On the slopes and off, who you ride with is key to survival.

I've been pleasantly surprised by who I've met out here through the years. Today, I have the surreal privilege of touring mostly with expert queer and Black and Latine riders. My latest crew remind me of my first, a life-keeping mixture of keen observation, serious discussion, and playful whimsy. We freestyle in parking lots as on our boards, we cackle freely in the woods, endlessly clown each other over clumsy mistakes, and gas each other up to fully send that long-coveted trick. Our conversations are just as bodacious and vulnerable, too, ranging from stories of destination riding in Chile and the French Alps to discussing whether our hitchhiking attempt failed (or succeeded) because of skin color. We are ever grateful for the community, each of us having carved similar lines through rocky social exchanges to make it out here. Our numbers, like our camaraderie, felt like an eternal win. My crew and I fell in love with couloirs and started to learn to ice climb, so together we move ever upward.

And some things haven't changed; the backcountry has its constants. Every time I'm out here, I relearn that mortal threats are the only rational things to fear. I relearn that, because virtually no one belongs out here, I actually fit in. Every time, it's love reignited. Out here, I live and embody my dreams, they themselves the size of mountains. All that I hope for and all that I long to be feels tangible and close. If I can get out into those mountains, pick a line, and make it home safely, I can do anything.

TWIRLING IN NATURE

LeeLee James

With my cassette player in my pocket, walking the back streets to avoid gangs and the stares of those sitting in rush hour traffic, my younger self escaped to another plane. I dreamed big and looked to the clouds as my fingers twittled and snapped to the beat of my favorite jams. Still a bit shy, I would wait until the coast was clear before breaking out the choreography I'd stayed awake memorizing. The breeze was so reliable, always coming at the right time, right on cue, at the climax, after the bridge, while crossing the bridge over the highway.

I discovered freedom from my surroundings, a way to escape my trauma. I kept that routine daily, got straight A's in school, and won my ticket out of the hotbed of the post–Jim Crow South, which was reeling from the crack epidemic of the early '90s. There, I found balance. When the central air conditioning had frozen my soul, I could escape to the out-of-doors to be recharged. It would be the start of a formative relationship, a reliance on the Twirl. Only she knew how to straighten me out, and I would come to dwell in her presence at difficult times throughout my life.

More than a decade later, I found myself in a stiff gray office in downtown Denver. Following the weed boom, this dusty western city had become more diverse and presumably more progressive than ever before. Oh, this place was fancy, with these floor-to-ceiling glass walls, and even though I could see straight through to the receptionist, she still made me stand there in the hallway looking crazy until the hiring manager told her it was OK to let me in. See, gates aren't only for keeping things in; they're also for keeping things out. This gorgeous view of downtown and the open floor plan seemed like nice additions to an appealing salary and benefits package. Unfortunately, this interview would turn out to be whack, like so many others I'd had that year. I asked, "What kinds of initiatives does your company have for ensuring a diverse staff and environment?" My interviewer responded, "We like to make sure our employees know that if they want to take a Friday off, they are more than welcome to do so, as long as they get their work done."

It was obvious I was the first trans person some of these interviewers had ever met, but I wasn't expecting to be the first Black person they'd ever interviewed. Even so, this interview proved more palatable than the networking event I had gone to where the head of engineering laughed out loud when I asked about the diversity metrics for Black people. He smugly replied, "We don't know that." I could feel my blood beginning to boil and knew that I would need to **twirl**—to shed the feelings of erasure and cleanse my soul of the generations of trauma welling up inside me triggered by that dismissive response. I could hear the wind chimes calling me outdoors to release my pain and anguish.

I first twirled through my hometown, Memphis, Tennessee. I experienced varying levels of violence both at school and, unfortunately, at home. At fifteen years old, when I was old enough to walk between the two places, I discovered this new form of healing. My walks were my time alone and fed a need for agency that I'd been disallowed. While jamming out to Deborah Cox on my cassette player, left to my own whimsy, I became meditative and aware. As I was walking home at 3 p.m., it was especially quiet in the neighborhood, as most parents were still at work or beginning their commutes through the big city.

This was a ripe opportunity for my shy self to **twirl** to my heart's content. Arms overhead, surrendering to the waves of emotion that washed over me, I would sing at the top of my lungs like I did in the back rows of church, as if only the Lord could hear me. I twirled through the pain, away from the gaze of the Evangelical Christian, cis-het (cisgender-heterosexual) normative people who inhabited every other facet of my life. To further escape that gaze and grow my agency, I relocated to Alaska after I graduated from high school.

I found a new sense of value in the outdoors, in having the space to be alone and simply exist in my humanity. I've used outdoor spaces to process so much trauma, free of charge, and to plot so many victories as well as meditate on manifestation. Naturally, being in Alaska catalyzed a love for mountain landscapes and tree-lined trails. I've had the privilege of hugging trees from the Cascades to the Great Smokies and have twirled from the Alps to the Alaska Range, giving mother nature a little performance in appreciation for her hospitality. I enter her gates broken and leave whole again. Twirling is the love language I use with myself, a check-in between self and universe where I evaluate if I'm where I need and want to be. In the spaciousness, I can hear and receive my heart's honest answers. "Don't give up," my heart says. "You are everything you're looking for." Message received. My posture then corrects, and with a deep inhale I straighten my back, head held high, and press forward to try and break barriers for yet another day.

After a year of pointless coding challenges and cringeworthy software engineering interviews, it had become clear to me that my skills alone would not be enough to land me my first role in tech. You see, I had bought into the sales pitch that after attending the Turing School of Software and Design (a seven-month-long coding boot camp), I would get a job in the industry within a year of completing the program. However, six months after the program ended, everyone in the class except me had secured near six-figure contracts at respectable start-ups and tech companies. I had a different experience from the rest of my cohort and blamed myself for a long time. Why did I need to be different? Why did I have to be unconventional? Why couldn't I be basic enough for these people to invest in me and my ability to bring value to their team? My twirls told me that I was valid and worthy, so why did the world, the universe, not agree?

Having recently retired from touring as a professional figure skater, I knew how to ham it up at networking events, how to command a room, make friends, dress nice, start conversations, and dazzle a crowd. After tutoring some of my classmates and watching them go on to get jobs, I was confident in my skill. I stopped blaming myself and started asking, "What gives?"

Even writing about this experience unveils a great deal of pain and frustration about the disapproval I felt as a person trying to fit into a landscape that never intended to add my portrait to its canvas. Seven months after the program's end, my money started to run out; I had racked up credit card debt trying to make this dream a reality. I went for a fabulous twirl through the trees, where I laid my burdens down and made a promise to myself that after nine months of trying, I would go back to college and get my bachelor's degree in computer science. I got confirmation from the breeze, and with my heart rate lowered, I was able to see my plan B. Nine months is long enough to have a baby and completely change your life, so if my circumstances were going to change, it could happen in that window of time. The day before the deadline to apply for college admissions—at nine and a half months, lo and behold!—I got accepted. I was about to turn thirty-five years old and start a new career from scratch, but this active decision to keep moving forward excited and energized me.

I returned to the world of academia in Boulder, Colorado, which is touted as heaven on earth for anyone who enjoys the outdoors. On the campus of CU Boulder, I had anticipated feeling some relief from the year I had just experienced. I'd be starting over, on the ground floor, where everyone had the same chance at success. Much to my surprise, there was a lot of work still to be done within myself and the community that I was now paying an ass-load of money to be a part of. Forms of gatekeeping, bias, sexism, classism, and ageism similar to those I'd experienced while on the job hunt were alive and well in this bright, shiny new institution. It troubled me that I could see people like me at drag shows at night but then be the sole reflection of my people during the day. The "aha" moment for me came when I was speaking with a notably woke, respectful professor of robotics about strengthening accessibility and representation within tech. When I suggested that he pull from his mother's experiences as a point of reference, he turned to me and asked, "How is my mom underrepresented in tech?" To which I replied, "I'm assuming that she's a woman, but I could be wrong."

He and I were both floored by his apparent disconnect from identity and the disparity of visibility concerning anyone who didn't share his identities. That called for a twirl. In being disappointed by my expectations of him, I realized that I needn't wait for someone else in order to actualize the purpose in my own heart, nor to recognize and acknowledge it. I needed to actualize that purpose for myself.

So that is exactly what I did, starting with my final project for my Wearable Technologies course. I used the assignment as a launching pad to start my YouTube channel, where I shared the technologies I used in my university coursework. I couched my experiences in a relatable and fun way for people who look like me, Black queer and trans femmes who might also want to code or program robots, because why not? I wanted to pay homage to the twirls that gave me such agency and access to my own imagination by culminating each episode out in nature, merging the technological and natural worlds.

I blew that project out of the water. After only ten months I had close to fifteen hundred subscribers (and I am grateful for every one of them), with my channel highlighted on YouTube's Instagram feed. From this boom, I've landed paid partnerships with Meow Wolf, an arts and entertainment company that creates large-scale interactive and immersive art installations, and Visible (a subsidiary of Verizon). I then launched a successful Patreon campaign that funds the continuation of my work, like a series of personalized videos I've dropped entitled *The Climb*. In the series, I take viewers adventuring with me around some of the most breathtakingly beautiful, twirlable, and accessible national parks in America.

By becoming a business owner in my sophomore year, I learned that I don't want to work for some white man in a start-up. In fact, I want to be the boss. I am forced to believe in myself every day, as I am responsible for maintaining the work I've created, work celebrated by people like Jason Mraz and Angelica Ross who feel a resonance with me, my experience, and my vision for the future. I use my resources—even those gatekept by systems and institutions that have historically existed to block people like me—to build fervor and assiduously face my imposter syndrome head on. I have become a specialist on the future self I know I want to arrive at and the work she will be doing. With credentials no longer the be-all and end-all, my purpose-driven life is motivation enough. None of this would have been possible if I did not know that I can learn anything and do anything, one twirl at a time.

The same Black girl who started teaching herself to ice skate at nineteen years old and then proceeded to twirl the world as a professional figure skater for the better part of a decade has an unmatched growth mindset. Because of that girl, I'm confident that when I finish what I've set out to do here, I will twirl to look within and survey my value. So I raise my glass and make a toast: **Cheers to me!** The baddest bitch in every building I enter and the Amazonian goddess in every forest I meander. I no longer seek validation from a hiring manager at Twitter. It's quite clear why no one hired me that year. They were afraid of the power I hold—and they should be, because I'll twirl on a hoe.

WALKING ANCESTRAL PATHS

TOGETHER WE TURN

Avani Skye Fachon

One turn around,
and another,
and another . . .

———

It is dusk, and I twirl on the veranda in my grandmother's old crimson-red swivel chair. A bag of six precious tamarind balls is crumpled in my hand, sugar crystals scattered across the tiles. As I turn—around and around and around—textures of light, scent, and sound dance, prod-ucts of this garden nestled in Kingston, Jamaica. One turn around—soft dots of pink from the crown of thorns (*Euphorbia milii*) and desert roses (*Adenium obesum*).[1] Another turn—a whiff of sweet Julie man-

---

1 Names often reflect our sense of place and belonging, embodying our knowledge about or revealing our relationship to a species. Some names are linked to the appearance, behavior, and cultural importance of an organism. Others can shed light on the relation-ship between different creatures and the evolutionary history that formed their unique identities. Names can also reflect troubling pasts—memories of foreign expedition spon-sors or collectors who used unethical methods to gather their samples, for example. Names are direct evidence of the memory and identity of a species through human eyes,

goes (*Mangifera indica*) fallen to the ground. Yet another—the familiar, recurrent song of a pea dove (*Zenaida aurita*), *cooOOoo-coo-coo-coo*. As I turn, here amidst the rhythm of the family garden, I soak in this environment's overflowing memory bank—a natural record of history, connection, and ecopersonal[2] identity.

Light blankets distant stars, and sleeping dogs (Canis familiaris) twitch their ears. Above the chair, a house spider (Araneae sp.) tunes its web, diligently adjusting the tension and stiffness of the silk.

Morning sun scatters shadows through the ornate iron grate and onto glossy white tiles, forming a kaleidoscope at my feet as I spin. Ellipses of sugar ants (*Camponotus* sp.) twist through outlines of light and dark, making their way to gather fallen sucrose. The thin ant lines resemble strands of hair on the attic floor of my grandmother's 1960s Watford, England, home as she gave her customers the latest styles. Back then, the chair spun, too, each time revealing a smiling face in the mirror as the Black women customers admired new coiffures, hot combed into curly bobs or pinned up into beehives. At such times, the chair turned as the women absorbed the comfort of the attic—my grandmother's care as she handled their tresses, a soft humming of familiar songs, a sense of community often missing amidst the racism and discrimination of England's gray streets.

A newly formed chrysalis is sheltered under a dewy branch of the pear tree (Persea americana, also known as avocado). Deep within, imaginal discs—fueled by the pulpy meltdown of a caterpillar's body—awaken. At first, the caterpillar's immune system resists these previously dormant,

---

and of our own intertwined identity and relationship to nature. In the effort to document these complexities, this piece records local, common, and scientific names.

2 I am using "ecopersonal" to refer to the ways in which local ecosystems impact and shape personal identity. Here, I explore my ecopersonal identity in relation to my Afro-Caribbean heritage. Each person has an ecopersonal identity that has been intricately formed over multiple temporal and spatial scales, whether conscious of it or not.

mysterious cells, grappling against the unknown. But it is soon revealed that these discs contain a detailed blueprint for building the butterfly's external structures. A tarsus, a wing scale, a compound eye—these dreamers rouse, multiply, and clump, carrying out plans for a grand metamorphosis, the link between an old identity and a new one on an early morning.

When my grandmother returned to Jamaica in 1968, the chair endured the crests and troughs of waves rocking the cargo ship on its journey across the Atlantic, the vessel coated with Sahara dust swirled up into the atmosphere by seasonal transatlantic winds. Later, from its new home on the Kingston veranda, looking out to the yard, the chair sat amidst slow cycles of evolution, as organisms adapted and adjusted to thrive in the garden's embrace, taking on new identities—fruits becoming smaller and sweeter in drought; trees altering their blossoming and fruit set; some species finding more comfort in higher altitudes, outside of the garden's boundaries, others finding more comfort within; some changing their colors, structures, and behaviors—ever so slightly—to better survive in the fluctuating environment. It witnessed rhythms of photosynthesis and respiration; cycles of bloom, pollination, and growth; patterns of decomposition and nutrient fixation; hatching, cocooning, and molting; annual migrations across the bright night, guided by ever-forming, aging stars and the waxing-waning moon. It witnessed animated, hand-clapping game songs, visits from the ice cream bicycle man, and long conversations under the mango tree. It noticed as garden visitors were edified by the spines coating a soursop fruit (*Annona muricata*), the soft flutter of a cloudless sulphur butterfly (*Phoebis sennae*), and the peck-pecking of a Jamaican woodpecker (*Melanerpes radiolatus*, endemic) at an open pod of ackee (*Blighia sapida*, national fruit). The chair detected the garden not as quiet and sleepy, as it initially appears to many passersby, but knotted with a life and recollection that reverberate over space and time.

Over the years, the chair and its occupants have turned in interconnected cycles as nature turns, as memory turns, as identity turns.

A brown anole lizard (Anolis lineatopus) *conducts a midday evaluation of the veranda from its picture frame perch. It has lost its tail, an act of self-amputation performed upon encountering a predator or extreme stress. Through resilience and regeneration, microscopic cycles within its cellular system are taking charge, growing its tail back for another day.*

Still another turn. The crimson chair squeaks. I used to mail my grandmother red fall leaves from Colorado sugar maples (*Acer saccharum*) pressed inside cards, knowing that she would appreciate a token of North American seasonal spectacle. She put the leaves away for safe keeping and called to tell about the juicy, elliptical-shaped leaflets she picked from the leaf of life (*Kalanchoe pinnata*) that flourishes below her bedroom window. Around the world, the species is known by myriad names: in Brazil, *folha-da-fortuna* (Portuguese for "fortune-leaf"); in the Philippines, *katakataka* (Filipino for "amazing"); in India, *amarapoi* (Odia for "deathless plant"); and in Puerto Rico, *yerba de bruja* (Spanish for "witch's weed"). Each name references its mysterious, highly resilient, and adaptable nature, as well as its array of medicinal uses. My grandmother places the leaves on wet newspaper, and little roots twist out of the fleshy ridges, exploring their new environment. Just like that, a piece of her garden takes root once again—a new cycle beginning, a continued spin of the chair and the ever-changing Kingston yard.

*A doctor bird (*Trochilus polytmus, *also known as red-billed streamertail; national bird and endemic) is busy feeding in the afternoon sun, injecting its long beak to draw sweet sips of nectar out of a pink desert rose, superfuel as its wings deftly flap in a figure-eight motion, over and over. Fine grains of pollen, the width of a hair, stick to the doctor's beak and iridescent feathers. Together, they travel to other flowers in the* *garden and beyond—a journey critical to upholding and strengthening the garden's web.*

I pop another tamarind ball into my mouth, reveling in the sweet and sour flavor as I push off to wheel around even faster. Young tamarind leaves (*Tamarindus indica*) fold in the absence of light, a mechanism believed to aid water conservation and protect against herbivory. Introduced to Jamaica centuries ago, the tree is often found along bumpy country roads or providing shade in public grounds and yards. Day after day, month after month, year after year, the tamarind tree has observed communities around it, following sweet-sour stories of jubilation and tribulation, freedom and constraint, love and violence—witnessing history. To restore and protect itself, it must close each night, each day opening to a new island chronicle. There are no tamarind trees in my grandmother's garden, so before returning to Colorado, my mother and I walk to the nearby supermarket and purchase small packets of tamarind balls to tuck into our suitcases. For weeks afterward, we ration the tamarind, savoring it—each ball carefully rolled in sugar and stories.

Dusk turns to night. The distant stars are revealed once again. The columnar cactus (Cereus *sp.) by the front gate stands tall and composed, faithfully guarding the driveway. Slowly, its large white flower opens like a beaming watchlight. The moon, too, is full tonight. Together, the two gentle eyes gaze across the garden, the veranda, the turning chair, and to my grandmother, inviting her to join a new cycle of life. She passes away peacefully into the night.*

Yet another turn, and I catch glimpses of yellow from the jimbilin tree (*Averrhoa carambola*) on the far end of the garden. Slicing horizontally through the fruit's waxlike skin reveals light flesh and glowing stars. I stretch up and reach as far as I can to pick one from a high branch. *Starlight, star bright, first star I see tonight.* The plump peel and pulp are packed with vitamins, minerals, and antioxidants. *I wish I may, I wish*

I might, have this wish I wish tonight. My five fingers are outstretched and extending with all their might toward that ripe, brilliant star calling my name. *I wish I may, I wish I might. . . .* The tree is laden with fruit and nourishing wishes, rooting me on through cycles of life. The jimbilin tree, the garden, and its diverse inhabitants provide a natural community of support, not unlike that found in the little Watford attic where this crimson chair once spun.

The air is becoming cooler. I feel dizzy for a moment, while the anansi house spider becomes stationary on its carefully tuned web, spying on the garden's secrets and vibrations. The garden exhales, and I inhale, each breath and bloom forging an ecopersonal history and identity, narratives of migration and mixed culture, of interspecies memory and connection, of glowing dreams that continue to live uniquely in the present and future. Once more, I am in balance.

A turn again, and the dog lifts an ear as the elliptical leaf of life outside my grandmother's window bestows upon us its rare bloom. With all of its hidden gifts, the species has still another name: cathedral bells. Pinkish red chimes are aligned in branched clusters. How heartening—always another spin, another turn, another cycle, another strand of the web. And there is a way in which I can still feel my grandmother in the currents of a doctor bird's beating wings and in the morning sunlight; in the sweet smell of Julie mango, in the Colorado autumn leaves, in a newly formed chrysalis, and amongst the stars. Together, we sit out on the veranda, and she squeezes my leg, tight-tight, feeling my flesh and bones, relishing the sweet-sour Kingston breeze turning through the cycles of the bright night.

. . . and another turn,
and another . . .

DREAMS OF HOME

Dr. Tanisha M. Williams

I have always wanted to travel throughout Africa. The stories of people of African descent in the Americas do not begin in the stolen lands of the Americas. I grew up learning about the many beautiful places, people, cultures, and traditions across the African continent. Learning this rich history gave me a longing to go home—the place my ancestors were torn away from.

As a child, I read all I could about the continent and its people, my people. I would look at pictures in our encyclopedia for hours, just mesmerized. I even asked my great-grandmother on several occasions if we could move to the continent (Ghana, in particular). She said, "No, our life is here." I then asked if we could move to the Caribbean, also no. So Washington, DC, is where we stayed, but I never gave up trying to move us. The land I knew was part of my history, but I always had a dream of returning to the land I never knew.

When I reached the Motherland for the first time in 2014, the feeling of setting my feet firmly on the continent, this place I had longed to be, hit me like a ton of bricks. I was stepping onto the lands I had read and dreamed about for so long. This feeling of returning home is not unique to me. Many people of African descent have expressed similar feelings about their first time on the continent. It is the collective recognition of being home—our ancestral home, my ancestral home—and that we are also foreigners to a place we should know well. The feeling also carries the (generational) trauma of being taken from the land and then returning to it with a slight sense of familiarity and yet so much distance, disconnect, and exclusion.

I remember landing after the seventeen-hour flight and gathering my things for the journey to my housing for the night. I wearily walked off the plane at the airport in Cape Town, South Africa, and then I saw the words "Welcome to the Mother City" on a large sign written in stone. Reading that sign, I lost my breath and became choked with emotions. I had finally made it **home**.

My journey to South Africa was for work. I was conducting my dissertation research on a number of native plant species from the genus *Pelargonium* L'Hér. (family Geraniaceae). We affectionately call them pellies in my lab, but you may know them as scented geraniums (although many are not really geraniums, which is a separate genus). I was, and still am, trying to understand if these plants could adapt and respond to climate change impacts such as changes in temperature and shifts in rainfall.

In doing this work as a botanist and ecologist, I explored a lot of the coastal regions of South Africa alone. These long drives and weeks in the field gave me time to think, read, and reflect on not only my scientific research but also my emotional and spiritual growth. My time spent in South Africa was transformative. Some of that transformation can be attributed to seeing Black people thrive and experience true joy. I don't know the words to describe it, but I felt more relaxed about smiling, laughing, and being myself. Some of it was learning from colleagues and friends from places outside of the US and outside of Eurocentric spaces. And some of it was learning more about the similarities and differences between Jim Crow in the US and apartheid in South Africa. These lessons were among the hardest. It doesn't matter where you are in the world, there are histories (and current events) of trauma to Black, Indigenous, and other people of color.

The hope I got from going to Robben Island, Soweto, the Apartheid Museum, and other historical sites was not only from the fact that people persevered and resisted, as we always do; it was also from the stories of reconciliation. Reconciliation does not mean justice, but it is a way to uncover some truths. The South African Truth and Reconciliation Commission (TRC) met from 1995 to 2002. The commission was established as a way to "heal from the past" and help the country move forward through uncovering the truth about gross human rights violations committed during apartheid (1948 through 1994). This type of national recognition of wrongdoing and engagement struck a chord with me. What would happen if we saw more of these reconciliation commissions? What would that look like in the US? All of these new experiences and information helped me learn more about the plants, people, and cultures of South Africa, but also more about my own views, culture, and sense of belonging in spaces.

Many amazing stories come to mind when I think about my four years in South Africa. I think about Kirstenbosch National Botanical Gardens, a place where I was honored to work and have a research garden. I think about the University of Cape Town and Cape Peninsula University of Technology, where I worked. I think about the Mowbray neighborhood, where I met many of my best friends. I think about the many lectures, seminars, concerts, dining experiences, museums, festivals, volunteer events, hikes, and good fun I enjoyed while living in such a vibrant place. What always comes to mind are plants, plants, plants. South Africa has the sixth largest number of plant species in the world and is the most species-rich country on the continent. It is a botanist's dream!

When I think about plants, I first think about my pellies and my many field excursions. (They were like scavenger hunts!) I was equipped with

maps, GPS points, felt tip pens, a field notebook, a measuring tape, speci-
men baggies, calipers, a hand lens, and sunglasses. I would hike and drive
along roadsides looking for a glimpse of the sage-to-almost-lime-green
leaves or the white, pink, or purplish flowers. My greatest success was
finding a population of the lovely *Pelargonium capitatum* along a cliff
overlooking the Atlantic Ocean. It was one of the most beautiful field
sites I have ever visited. I did my measurements of the plants and then
sat down near them. I admired the sight of my pellies dancing in the
ocean breeze. I was taken aback for a moment realizing that this is what I
get to do for a living. I felt really grateful that I get to wake up and attempt
to understand what the plants are telling us about their history, their
current ecology, and how they are responding to the rapid changes to
their environments. I love this line of inquiry. What is our environment
and the species living within it trying to tell us? If we could slow down
and listen, we might begin to learn how to overcome some of the complex
issues we have created for ourselves.

On other days I would park my small white rental car at Kirstenbosch
National Botanical Gardens' side gate, flash my permit, and head to one
of my research gardens. It would be a long day of measuring plants, weed-
ing, and taking pictures, but I got to do it in the world's most beautiful
botanic garden. Being alone in nature doing repetitive work—measuring
plant height, leaf width and length, and number of flowers—gave me time
to think. As I measured, wrote, measured, I was able to contemplate my
wishes of seeing the continent as a child and how far I had come. I would
think about my work and its usefulness to conserving plants in South
Africa. As I got into a rhythm of measuring, I would veer off and think
about the many people I had the opportunity to work with, learn from,
and call family.

Years have passed since I got back from South Africa. A number of
moments in 2020 during the pandemic shifted or made clear what I

want to do with my life and career. I realized that community building is one way to combat some of the issues surrounding climate change, justice, equality, and freedom. During the height of the lockdown and in between the brutal murders of Black people in the US, an online community began to form. Black Birders Week was started in response to the bird-watching incident in Central Park. Although I am not a birder, I participated in this week. When I saw people who looked like me, Black people enjoying nature in a variety of ways, it brought joy to my heart.

I wanted the same accessibility, visibility, and feeling of belonging brought to the plant science / botanical space. I sent out a Tweet asking if Black people who love plants wanted to work on making a similar movement. And so Black Botanists Week was born on June 8, 2020. The Black Botanists Week committee consists of eleven acclaimed Black botanists plus me. We are teachers, illustrators, photographers, authors, academics, houseplant enthusiasts, foragers, and everything in between. We like to say our committee is as diverse as the plants we love.

Being part of the Black Botanists Week committee made me reflect on the lack of representation of Black people in botanical fields and made me want to highlight all those who are thriving as Black botanists. I thought about how growing up I never had Black botanist role models. During the first year of Black Botanists Week, we changed the definition of who a botanist is to anyone who loves plants, wanting to include those like houseplant enthusiasts and farmers who are often not looked upon as botanists. We strongly acknowledge that you don't need a college degree to be a botanist, you just need a love for plants. With this shift in thinking and inclusion, I am starting to see that I have known some amazing Black botanists along my path. The first Black botanist I knew was my great-grandmother, Grace Alice Hawkins, who was a registered nurse and had a knack for making our home feel like a plant oasis.

South Africa is where I got to work and learn from so many Black botanists. There were professors, researchers, students, farmers, and conservationists that I met along the way. Not until writing this piece did I realize how blessed I am to have had so many great examples of Black people loving, caring for, and conserving plants.

THE JOY AND PERSISTENCE OF THE BLACK FISHER TRADITION

Camille Mosley

For Granny, Mom, and Dad

When I reflect on my memories in nature, I most often recall the innumerable hours I've spent near water. "Water is life" is not a catchy phrase to be used lightly. It resonates with me when I think about my family history in coastal Mississippi. The Gulf transformed my identity, imagination, and worldview. A snapshot of the landscape would show natural scenes of birds onshore, my feet submerged in greenish waves, and soft yet faceted sand awaiting transformation into castles. These environmental scenes hold many stories and histories unseen.

The art of fishing has existed globally as a source of livelihood and relaxation for centuries. With 3.2 billion people relying on fish for protein, fish consumption is growing faster than animal consumption.

African fishing has a rich and extensive history, thanks to the diversity of cultures and ecosystems that span its coasts. Time-honored fishery traditions are integral components of artisanal fishers' lives. Memories, friendships, and food are uniting themes in the daily life of African fishers. And this ingrained, longstanding tradition was present when Black people were kidnapped and held captive by white colonials.

As Africans were brought to the United States, fishery culture persisted. Many groups of African captives were transplanted to the coastlines of North America. To survive in a foreign and hostile landscape, our ancestors returned to the fishery traditions of their homelands. They used their experiential knowledge to gather resources by subsistence fishing, trapping, and farming the land. Not only did fishers retain their tradition, but they also directly contributed to their livelihoods by providing food for their communities. Continual communion with the environment persisted through the evil violence of slavery in North America. From the fishermen in Pointe à la Hache on the Gulf coast to the Gullah Geechee people on the Atlantic coast, African Americans have contributed immeasurably to commercial and recreational fishing through their participation in the workforce and economy.

African Americans created seafood-based Southern cuisines still eaten today on the Gulf of Mexico, like in the small town where my grandmother settled. The daily life of citizens, including meal preparation, an activity of necessity yet also leisure in many Black households, was almost always influenced by the Gulf. Food was a significant unifying theme in the community. Gumbo—my absolutely favorite dish—is a soup made with shrimp, crabmeat, sausage, vegetables, and a myriad of spices served atop a bed of rice. With origins in the West African *soupe kandia*, or okra soup, gumbo was brought to North America by African captives through their food tradition and their traditional ecological knowledge of how to grow the vegetable. Gumbo was a mainstay in our house and across the coastal US South, most often associated with Louisiana cuisine. Going to get shrimp po'boys and boiled crayfish from the renowned Bozo's is a treat I still enjoy today. The fresh local seafood and seasoned expertise of the shop makes every bite worthwhile. These treasures from nature feed our body and soul. Treasure hunting—activities like fishing and crabbing—is a livelihood and recreational pastime for everyone here.

Africans and African Americans also influenced American culture and art through basket weaving and through pronounced musical rhythms that are still heard in many genres of music, including R&B and jazz. Our deep connection to nature, which aided persistence and cultural preservation in the midst of unimaginable hardship, was at stake with the retaliation for the abolishment of slavery. White Southerners felt defeated and threatened by the new freedoms of their Black compatriots. Their ignorance and unabashed hatred manifested in a set of rules and regulations for newly freed people referred to as the black codes. The codes were tools to reinstate control by wealthy white Southerners over people and labor. Particularly, the black codes restricted any means of resource harvesting, explicitly banning fishing and hunting, with the intention to undermine Black survival. The privilege of recreation and the sometimes-necessity of using natural resources for sustenance were stolen with no way to retrieve them without violence. Fishing, an activity that most people see today as an unbiased and nonracial pastime, was weaponized against Black Americans.

Growing up in the coastal South taught me that there was a space for us Black people in nature. I experienced firsthand the joys of treasure hunting with my family. A familiar and frequent event for us was to fish from dusk to dawn on the pier under the bridge. Bait for the crab nets included shrimp, freshly caught small fish, and raw chicken. From my elementary school days, I recall filling up a cooler to the brim with cherished blue crab. My nine-year-old self felt immensely small next to this trough of seafood. It felt as if this bounty were bestowed on us by a magical process, but it was actually garnered with the skill and patience of Mother, who was at the helm of the crabbing operation. Fishing was a sport that involved ancestral and natural histories. I delighted in my father's stories of fishing trips past and tried my hardest to sponge all the experiential knowledge, the tips and tricks of the game. Despite this childhood, I still didn't grasp how important fishing was to my presence with nature and connection to my ancestors until the oil spill happened.

Our families had just started to recover from Hurricane Katrina, which flooded my grandmother's home, when the BP *Deepwater Horizon* oil spill disrupted our livelihoods. The spill happened before I understood the concepts of climate change, capitalism, and environmental racism. I thought the ocean was impenetrable. No sea wreck or beach construction could alter my mental image of the Gulf, the ever-abounding treasure trove. My brain couldn't comprehend that the vast and beautiful blue-green expanse of the Gulf was in danger. Feeling surprise and heartbreak, twelve-year-old me tried to wrap my brain around how this could happen and how we could fix the devastation. My body ached with a sense of disbelief and trepidation at the changes to come for our coastal lifestyle.

The news bellowed sentiments of sadness, calls to action, and reserved resilience in the significant environmental aftermath of this blow. Chemical dispersants, framed as a cure in the moment, devastated the bodies of marine creatures. Every organism in the ecosystem, including humans, relied on the ecosystem services of the Gulf, and Black Gulf communities relied on the water for mental reprieve, sustenance, and transport, but these connections were tarnished and severed. Fishing life was irrevocably halted, and the local fishers felt a weight heavy on their hearts and homes. Recreational fishing became hazardous because the seafood was deformed, untested, and bacteria ridden. Suddenly, news of dolphins washing up on the beach became a regular occurrence. The beach shorelines were patterned with balls of tar besides the usual human debris. We shifted our harvest fishing to releasing every fish caught, which felt like a tease after being in the habit of filling up coolers for dinners to come. The peaceful, majestic visage of the shoreline was no more.

Promises of compensation and a return to "normalcy" were met with skepticism, but the Gulf communities didn't have much choice or many options for relief. Quite a few of our families had members who worked as ship crew, shrimpers, oystermen, or fishers, and/or owned seafood shops. The economy suffered, and for many folks scraping by, this was the last straw, resulting in family relocation and job changes. Finding ways to make a living in the area was already a struggle in Mississippi, the poorest state in the United States. Because of the local economy, many folks decided to get hours of work helping with beach cleanups and dispersal crews. No good deed went unpunished, as they would be exposed to hazardous chemicals, even under instruction and "protective gear." Humans weren't the only terrestrial creatures who suffered these new harms. Coastal bird species like the endangered sandhill crane relied for survival on aquatic creatures such as snails and crayfish in marshy savanna habitats upstream. Over the years, it seemed that matters only continued to get worse for living things on land and in the sea.

Once seafood and the water were deemed safe by officials, my family, like many others, reentered our sacred spaces on the Gulf. Some familiar characteristics remained: the salty air with a crisp and shrimpy finish greeted our noses onshore. These waterways feeding into the Gulf were our favorite fishing spots. From the mix of freshwater and saltwater treasures, the brackish channels gave up mysterious and unexpected finds. We returned to the dependable pier below the Pascagoula River bridge, where we could fish for hours and hours with what felt like an infinite bounty, but the action and harvest was now slow. At the place where I had caught two fish on one rod before I hit puberty, I had extreme difficulty getting even a bite. After quick conversation with fellow fishers on the platform, my father delivered the tough verdict that things, even years after, had still not recovered. Crabbing, an activity that rivaled my love for hook and line fishing, became an abysmal practice. The nets would collect the signature feisty blue crabs, signaling to us that populations must be recovering, but looks were deceiving. We returned home with our bounty only to be affronted by oil-filled dead man's fingers (gills) when cleaning the harvest for gumbo. Witnessing environmental tragedy and its reverberations of harm in my community firsthand was crushing. I took the hurt from the spill and my transformed curiosity about fisheries to fuel my pursuit of science and research.

Before I moved away from the Gulf Coast, sometime after the spill as a tween, I went on a field trip to the National Oceanic and Atmospheric Administration (NOAA) office near town. During the excursion with my middle school classmates, I got to dissect sharks. My endless curiosity about and comfort with wildlife proved handy; as many classmates retreated at the unbearable smell, I couldn't get enough. We also had hands-on learning activities displaying how shrimp nets were engineered to protect turtles and other creatures caught up in the trawl. I realized then that this was another aspect of fisheries science I could immerse myself in. In high school, I started thinking about college options and what opportunities would make me happy and provide a life of stability. I kept being drawn to environmental science. When I reflected on my happiest childhood and young adult memories, they all involved the outdoors. I enjoyed science and continually learning about what's around us and within us.

Declaring an environmental science major was incredibly easy, but the work would prove trying. My undergraduate education at a private white-serving institution continued to display the systematic processes that often left me among the few Black people or the only Black person in the classroom. Knowing my connection to the environment and how outside traditions were engrained in Black culture, I was conflicted about belonging. As I transitioned to graduation and learned that I could study the sport I had participated in as a child, warm feelings and excitement reverberated through my being. The familiar sense of being outside and on the water confirmed my choice in graduate studies. When I visited the Gulf, which is still my grandmother's home, I became immersed in nostalgia about coastal life and nature's pain.

The spill did not alter the spirit of purpose of Black families in the coastal communities. Commitment to the environment and community is integral to the resilience of Black fishers in the Gulf. Even wounded groups still banded together to pursue legal ramifications of the blow. Commercial and recreational fishers and businesses continued to monitor the systems and record the progress and health of the fisheries. Word-of-mouth movements provided support to seafood shops and restaurants to keep these places open. The folks who had been displaced or had to change occupations preserved their history orally, through storytelling and photographs that detailed the hard work of our ancestors. Being removed from the coastal land developed by our ancestors is not uncommon in African American coastal communities.

The Harris Neck community and Gullah Geechee descendants rallied to get their land returned after the US government intruded on their coastal haven to establish an airfield. Descendants did not let their dispersal prevent them from uniting and making a stand. The contributions made by their ancestors in the oyster fisheries and economy are now forever documented in history through news, TV, and legal reports.

Our coastal communities must overcome the threats to our ecosystems from climate change, environmental degradation, and species invasion. Through all these environmental tragedies, Black coastal communities and fishers also have to participate in a background battle for their humanity. When advocating for our environment, we advocate for ourselves.

Moments of Black joy and environmental persistence are positive outcomes from the disaster. Gulf ecosystems are not pristine (and some argue that an ecosystem with humans can never be), but they are recovering from the spill. Coral reefs continue to live, and these areas are now federally protected from oil rigs and commercial fishing. A new species of whale was identified in the Gulf of Mexico in January 2021, and it may exist only in US waters. Marine biologists still haven't fully investigated this new species' ecology, but this discovery, like many others, opens opportunities for research and funding toward sustaining these coastal systems. The once-endangered sandhill crane population is now stable, and habitat expansion in the refuge area, funded by penalties from the spill, will aid in further population growth and establishment of nests. Similar to the resilience of African American coastal communities, coastal wildlife continues to survive and even thrive in the Gulf.

My personal love of and reverence for nature from my experiences on the Gulf Coast are manifested in a fulfilling livelihood. The twelve-year-old me, enraged and impassioned by the *Deepwater Horizon* spill, would be more than elated to know my current life path. My childhood memories and solid sense of the past have further propelled me to stay in the fisheries field and push for more representation of Black people in the enjoyment and study of nature. While collecting data for my dissertation research, I delight in the familiarity of smelling like fish, seeing the clear-to-brownish lake water moving in layers on a windy day, and feeling the muscle memory of casting my rod with the click of the reel.

In these moments when I daydream, I return to the Gulf right next to my family.

Now much more mature and taller than my elementary school self, I still feel just as small, if not smaller, in the natural world. What is different now is that the sense of smallness sits alongside the mighty force I feel when I consider my current contributions to uplifting Black voices and my impact on the sustainability of fish populations to come. Imagine the feelings my ancestors experienced when treasure hunting and how they might feel knowing the Black resilience seen in myself and others. Much in line with the leaders of the Black coastal communities, I work hard, with purpose, to achieve a truer representation and inclusion of Black people in the environment.

YOU SHOULD SEE ME NOW

Xorla Seyram Ocloo

My parents grew up in the rural town of Keta, located in the Volta Region of Ghana. My mother would recount stories of trudging through rising floodwaters to attend school every day. Some days, water would flood her home and she would have to lay sandbags in front of her door. Since the early twentieth century, the rising Volta River and sustained erosion have badly diminished the soils of Keta. The erosion eventually ate away the land under her house, causing it to collapse and leaving my family homeless. When missionary groups from the United Kingdom came to provide assistance to the people of Keta, their concern was, "Do you need more English-speaking teachers in your town?" rather than, "How can we help with the floods?" Even twenty years after hearing this story, I'm still disappointed when I think about it.

Living in Keta was not easy. Although my parents and my older sister had family around, surviving was difficult. There was no money to go to the hospital, not enough money for food, and no money for entertainment. Survival was key, which is why my parents left Keta with my sister and emigrated to the United States to support their families back home and the family they were expanding (adding me and my brother later on).

When they moved us to the great city of Chicago in the 1980s, it felt like a mistake. They knew no one, didn't have family by their side, and were surviving on an annual salary of $16,000 for a family of five. Although food and resources were available, money wasn't. Back home in Ghana, people thought we were rich because we lived in the States, but it was exactly the opposite. We lived in a 500-square-foot apartment, shopped using resold food stamps, and bought all of our clothes from the thrift store (before it was cool).

Nothing killed me more than witnessing my mother coming home from an exhausting day. Every evening, the smell of Bengay pervaded our apartment as she wrapped her knees and went to work to feed five mouths. As the last born, I felt helpless, almost as if I were contributing to the problem by simply existing. I wanted to help. I wanted us to not regret moving to the United States. And thus, at the early age of fourteen, I took my first job working with Chicago After School Matters, a nonprofit organization aimed at providing teens with opportunities to explore their passions while earning a small stipend. I chose to learn how to print, bind, and design books. I earned about $169 for the summer; half went to my savings account and the other half I used as my allowance, so it wasn't necessary to ask my parents for money. Every summer after that, I worked in different positions with Chicago After School Matters. I worked as a TV production intern, a video production intern, and a bricolage designer (creating a mural that is still up in the Uptown neighborhood). I took any opportunity to make money to go toward my future in order to help my family, even if it was an internship for a career path I did not plan to pursue. I continued seeking jobs to save up for college because I knew it would be difficult for my family to pay for it all. As I continued earning my own money, I was able to help my family financially.

When I got accepted to the University of Illinois, I already had a plan for how I was going to pay for college—through working at the dining hall and applying for scholarships. Though I hated working at the dining hall from 8 p.m. to 12 a.m., nothing stopped me from picking up more shifts at $7.25 an hour. Eventually all the shifts and scholarships I earned made it possible for my mom to pay for the rest of my college tuition. My efforts significantly eased the financial burden on my family. While balancing my job, I also prioritized my major. I decided to choose a major that challenged me to go outside of my comfort zone—ecology.

You see, growing up in a Ghanaian-American household in Chicago, I had no access to outdoor activities, and they were discouraged anyway due to cultural associations between the woods and negative superstitions. I couldn't stare at owls, I couldn't catch certain fish, and I definitely couldn't hike in the woods. Taking ecology courses challenged me to be a brave, fearless, agile critical thinker. I trekked through dense forests and splashed into streams to learn about plants and animals. I spent hours in the forest, either counting and identifying tree species to understand succession or observing animals to understand species diversity. I quickly learned that my favorite feeling in the world was being a small piece in a complex ecosystem.

Word got out rather quickly among my Black friends that I was into "white-people stuff." My friends would say, "Ecology? What is that? Does that mean you have to look for bugs and plants? Isn't that for white people?" My response was, "It's for me." Among my white classmates, I was the token in all of my ecology courses. I was the "city girl," but a proud one who was willing to explore the wilderness. Among my family members, I always found it difficult to describe exactly what I do—partly because I was not seeking a traditional career. I grew up hearing from my family that I had to "be somebody" or, in other words, become a medical doctor. That's the career that brought in money and would help my family. When I told my siblings, "I count mosquitoes and zooplankton and freshwater ponds," I was met with puzzled looks. When I explained that studying these communities can help us better understand mosquito assemblage and mosquito-borne diseases like malaria, I heard sighs of relief because these were issues they could relate to. Although they were supportive, I could tell they were concerned about what careers I could pursue with this major.

As I delved further into field ecology, I realized there was more to science than identifying organisms and that human perspectives mattered in the research. I first saw inequities in research as a visiting scholar at Cape Eleuthera Institute (CEI) in the Bahamas. I noticed that most of the research was being conducted by non-Bahamians. Nonlocal researchers tried to persuade Bahamians to eat venomous lionfish in order to save other Caribbean fish populations. Immediately, I thought back to my childhood memory of my mother telling me to put a specific fish back in the water because our culture forbade us to eat it. I kept thinking, What if Bahamians didn't want to eat lionfish? What if it wasn't part of their diet or it went against their culture? Local voices were rarely involved in the solutions posed by well-meaning outsiders. The science at CEI was missing key insights from the local peoples, and it sparked my interest in bridging the gap between nonlocal researchers and local groups in future projects. Research had to be conducted in a better way, which meant prioritizing the needs of local communities. But reaching this goal came with unforeseen obstacles.

During my first year as a PhD student, I was sure I wanted to do the kind of work in Africa that mattered to local people. I was certain I knew which lab I was going to join—the lab I had dreamed of being part of since my undergraduate years. But when I got to that lab's institution, everything that was promised to me was thrown out of the window. I was admitted into my program, it seemed, because it would break records. I came in with the biggest cohort they had ever had, and it was the first time they had three Black women join the program. Although I was clear about which lab I wanted to join, when I got there the head of the lab (the principal investigator or PI) did not show any interest in me as a student. What made matters worse was that **after** I accepted my admission, professors and other students began telling me that the PI was no good. I wanted to hear this while I was inquiring about the program. I wanted to hear this when I came for interviews—not a week after my arrival at my new PhD institution. Most of my cohort already had an idea of which PI they wanted to work with, so that meant I was going to struggle to find an advisor.

I struggled because there weren't many professors who had the same research priorities as me. I also struggled because of funding, something I thought would not be an issue until I arrived (another surprise). Like many other students with historically underrepresented identities, I was depressed and disconnected from my cohort, graduate program, and institution. I started questioning whether I even liked science. That frightened me. I watched as my two Black friends left the program, and I became the only Black person in my cohort. The token, again. Anytime I stepped on campus, I was met with a dark cloud that followed me closely wherever I went. Fortunately, my cohort mate, who is now one of my best friends, saw me struggling and directed me to their PI. That one meeting with this PI changed my entire academic trajectory. During the meeting he reminded me that I had a place in my program, at my institution, and in academia. He reminded me that he cared about my success and that he was going to help me reach my goals.

We started brainstorming projects and topics that I cared about. He knew I had an interest in people and the environment, so together we decided that I would develop a project that involved a multi-use aquatic plant. This plant has been known to feed animals, fertilize crops, and control pests but was not widely used in Africa. We decided to explore the possibility of using the plant, which was local, in Senegal. I was excited about this location because it was an opportunity to work in the West African region my family hails from.

When I arrived in Senegal to do a preliminary study, I was greeted by the intense rays of the sun on my skin. Chicago never reached temperatures close to what I had experienced in Ghana, so coming to Senegal was like being back in my home compound. Although the purpose of the trip was to conduct projects, I took my time to explore the culture and the land fully. I took off my shoes and walked barefoot, as I'd done in Ghana. I went to the nearby corner store or *boutique* to buy sugar, milk, and other foods as I'd done in Ghana. I participated in the tea culture, where after every meal we would spend hours brewing three shot glasses of tea, building friendships. I even learned how to make the Senegalese national dish, *thieboudienne* (also spelled *ceebu jen*) or rice with fish, which is similar to the original national dish of Ghana, jollof rice. Though I wasn't in Ghana, I felt at home because of the many similarities.

I was more comfortable as a researcher in Senegal. I, a Black woman, was conducting research among other Black people. For once, I didn't have to think about the color of my skin or how I was the only one. If I made a mistake or misspoke, I was never afraid of being judged. It was working in Senegal that helped me realize that there is space for me to be a successful researcher.

Still, my goal was to prioritize Senegalese ecological needs. Every day, I went to different villages to meet with the village chief. Our discussions later drifted to talking about our different lifestyles and how my stay in Senegal had been. I was comfortable talking to the chiefs. They were always generous. After each discussion, they would offer me thieboudienne to eat and Attaya tea to aid in digestion. As we continued building our relationships, we talked more about why I was there and what they needed help with. Overwhelmingly, almost all of the farmers mentioned that they wanted to pay less to grow rice or have higher yields. I decided that was going to be the topic of my dissertation and that I would test if the multi-use plant could decrease fertilizer costs while increasing rice productivity.

I wanted to have a team of Senegalese people to tackle this issue. Africans are rarely included in research conducted in the Global North. I wanted to show my colleagues that research that includes perspectives from local people is successful, revolutionary, and true. By including Senegalese voices, I learned more about their land, the people, and what was and wasn't working in their rice production practices. This information was critical to steering my project. Publication in academic journals was no longer important to me. It was more valuable to build knowledge with people and effectively communicate it back to them through face-to-face interactions.

When I left Senegal and arrived back in the United States, I had a new drive—to finish what I had started in Senegal. This goal was particularly important to me because the chiefs told me that researchers would often come for a few weeks on a field mission and never come back or follow up. I didn't want to do that, so I maintained my contacts in Senegal. I am now completing my seventh month in Senegal and have been loving every moment of it.

Looking back, I'm not sure where I would be if I hadn't taken a chance and declared ecology as my major. I'm still learning the best way to be an ecologist, the best way to be a researcher, and the best way to include and support Black people. My parents wanted me to "be somebody"—and I'm becoming the environmental social scientist I never saw when I first started. Being in this very moment, supporting my people, encouraging my people, makes me feel deeply fulfilled, humble, and hopeful for future young, aspiring Black scholars.

AFRO, SWEET AFRO

Boluwatife Olawale

Afro, O my Sweet Afro,
I will describe you as the origin of the human race. From Egypt to Ethiopia, the mother of civilization.

Discovered in the early seventh century was Leptis Magna in Libya, the largest city of the ancient region of Tripolitania, containing some of the world's best-preserved remains of Roman architecture.

In the north, dating back to the late twelfth and early thirteenth centuries, is the panoramic rock-hewn church known as Bete Giyorgis in Lalibela, Ethiopia.

Built during the fourteenth and early fifteenth centuries were three of western Africa's oldest mosques—Djinguereber (Djingareyber), Sankore, and Sidi Yahia in the city of Timbuktu located on the southern edge of the Sahara, then the Mali Empire.

How about the impressive Temple of Luxor? It provides a picture of the architectural and religious customs of ancient Egypt, as in the Avenue of Sphinxes and the Barque Shrine of the Theban Triad.

Seated in the eastern Serengeti Plain are the fossil remains of more than sixty hominids, in the Olduvai Gorge in Tanzania.

Located in southeastern modern-day Zimbabwe are the stone ruins of the African Iron Age city now known as Great Zimbabwe, once the center of a trade empire based on agriculture, cattle husbandry, and gold trading on the Indian Ocean coast.

The endless list of the spectacular historical sites of Sweet Afro also includes the House of Wonders in Zanzibar, Tanzania (Bayt al-Ajaib); the ruins of the industrial city of Meroë in the ancient kingdom of Kush; and historic Robben Island north of Cape Town, South Africa.

The catalog is incomplete without the three overwhelming pyramids of stone that have aroused curiosity for thousands of years. The great Egyptian pyramids at Giza, on the outskirts of Cairo, are precisely aligned to the north-south axis. These pyramids are among the greatest mysteries of all time.

The tally of your natural endowments—your innate resources, your natural spaces, and your valiant manpower; your wealth—can never be overestimated.

But look, Afro! Your mountains are burning and your trees are falling.

See! Desert is fast encroaching on your forest. What will you do to this fast-drying waterfall?

The once-raging ocean has gone silent. Even the tides are nowhere to be found.

The marketplace is desolate, the abundant oil is waning, the cocoa plantations are declining, the great nation is begging, and her people are suffering.

What is to be done to remedy this discourse that disregards unity?

Afro, where is thy strength?!

People of the Afro nation, where is your voice?

I have heard your story, I have read news of your victory, and I have witnessed your beauty.

Blessed with abundant natural resources, splendor, cultural values, and wealth, you are indeed naturally endowed, Sweet Afro. The innate wealth of Nigeria, the abundance of Tanzania: gold, crude oil, coal, diamonds, silver, gemstones, marble, bauxite, manganese, nickel, copper, soda ash, uranium, tantalite, natural gas, and salt. Your opulence is bottomless!

These, with your grace, kindness, innocence, and piety, spurred predation by your brother nations. Exquisite in your ways, considerate in your dealings, you have a big wide heart that is so accommodating. Your brother nations had a plan to expand their regions, they had aims to increase their wealth and boost their economy, and they saw you as a tool to achieve these purposes. But you were ignorant of their greedy plight. You were not expecting war, torture, or a disturbed tranquility. You got extorted, starting with the transatlantic slave trade that established the Afro diaspora region, which began with meeting with your chiefs, then slave trade bartering. This trade was centered in West Central Africa, the Bights of Benin and Biafra, and the Gold Coast. It progressed to more violent means, slave raids and abduction, as occurred in the Bissagos Islands, in the palm-oil-wealthy land of Opobo.

Your brothers transported your people, made them aliens to the foreign land, mentally deceived them. Made them think they are less than a person, that there are limitations to their capacities. They exploited the labor of your people and made them their agricultural mercenaries, farm laborers, domestic servants; made them do their dirt and laundry; made them build their bridges and buildings. They deceptively exchanged their manufactured goods (guns and gunpowder) for your invaluable raw materials to boost their economy.

Your brothers colonized your territory. They deceived your kings and chiefs, motivated by the greedy ambition of domination. The mighty and powerful King Jaja of the wealthy Opobo land was cruelly exploited; forceful claims were made on all of King Jaja's subjects and wealth. They mined your diamonds, crude oil, and coal; took your gold, gemstones, and silver. Oh Sweet Afro, foreigners tragically took your natural endowment. So dependent are they on your resources that these invaders touched your land and turned it to misery. They disrupted the climate, caused an atmospheric hullabaloo, a tampered confidence, strength with no self-authority.

Against all odds, you overcame!

You arose in all your strength and might, refused your brother's intimidation, did not submit to an inferiority complex. You shone in your radiant glory and fought for your liberty. You won! You redeemed yourself from slavery and colonization!

Sweet and lively.

Valiant and strong.

Graceful and glorious.

But why, dear Afro, does your strength seem to fail? Why do your glories appear to fade?

Could it be that you need righteous and selfless leaders to arise and rule? Could it be that you lack patriots who are bold enough to be relentless for your growth?

I have traveled your lands, explored your regions, and adventured through your wombs. The places I saw confirmed your affluence; the people there were exuberant and accommodating, and I felt the halo of your territories.

O Sweet Afro, you are a preeminent nation! A pulchritudinous abode for my soul. Gifted with inspiring natural attractions; with air that soothes, makes peaceful the weather, and makes the land flourish. When I voyaged through your regions in a large boat over water, I was in awe of the magical sites I visited. Those exceptional scenes blessed my memory with lasting retention.

The northern region offered me the phenomenal sight of the ancient city of Dougga in Tunisia; likewise the distinct Hoggar Mountains in Algeria and the architecture of Aswan city on the Nile River in Egypt. Sudd in South Sudan, with a vast floodplain befitting one of the largest tropical wetlands in the world. The apex of my adventure!

But Afro, O my Sweet Afro, don't you know that the desert is encroaching on your forests?

When I saw the landscape of the highest mountain in Africa, Mount Kilimanjaro in the eastern region, I was wowed. Similarly, I marveled at the topography of Stone Town in the Zanzibar Archipelago, and Ngorongo Crater and Serengeti National Park in Tanzania. Lake Malawi is indeed one of the deepest lakes in the world, and I fell head over heels in love with the sight of different species of catfishes and cichlids, impressive fish diversity in the lake. The view of wildlife in Simien Mountains National Park in Ethiopia slowed my pace. Swimming and fishing in the waters of Praslin Island in the Seychelles was so refreshing. The colorful autumn leaves of the Bwindi Impenetrable Forest in Uganda really cut a dash on me. In Mauritius, the forested mountain known as Le Morne Brabant that sheltered runaway slaves in past centuries drew me down memory lane and moved me, while the captivating underwater waterfall I saw at Le Morne Peninsula seemed impossible and lightened my mood.

Mount Nyiragongo in the Democratic Republic of Congo in your central region bewildered my heart with its offering of dangerously molten red fire and a feeling of frosty temperature at the same time. It is known to actively house the largest volumes of molten lava in the universe.

But Afro, O my Sweet Afro, don't you know that the mountains are burning?

Your western region is exquisite. Because of my enthusiasm for wildlife, I was delighted when I toured Yankari National Park in Nigeria and Kakum National Park in Ghana. I was smitten by the landscape of cliffs and sandy plateaus at Bandiagara (Land of the Dogons) in Mali. My expedition to Rhumsiki Rock in the Mandara Mountains in Cameroon, Lake Retba in Senegal, and Ganvie in Benin gifted me a lifetime of eidetic remembrance. I found the terrain of Rhumsiki Rock, known to have been created by volcanic plugs, to be unique. Lake Retba is memorable for its pink color, caused by *Dunaliella salina* algae. Ganvie is Afro's largest lake village, and the whole village is built on stilts, a very innovative and brilliant way of surviving.

The southern region was a place of retreat for me. I took a helicopter flight over Mosi-oa-Tunya, the famous Victoria Falls, which gave me a better view of the Zambezi River as it flows along the border between Zambia and Zimbabwe. I was mesmerized when I sighted the dotted skin of an Angola reed frog and a double-scaled chameleon at Tundavala Gap in Angola; the 2.2-meter (7,218-foot) elevation of the mountain almost made me try hiking. As I took a walk in the red dunes of Sossusvlei in Namibia, the floury sand beneath my feet got me feeling airy and light. When I saw the shipwrecks, old ruins, and quaint beach towns on the Skeleton Coast in Namibia, I wondered at how subtly time makes things that were once novel obsolete. At the Okavango Delta in Botswana, I was fascinated by the swirling patterns of lush vegetation. In Lesotho, the nonstop rhythm of Maletsunyane Falls cleverly cajoled me into choreographing. In Mozambique, the Bazaruto Archipelago, a group of six islands off the southern coast, got me wondering how this spectacle came into existence.

The real possibility of danger (robbery, kidnapping, murder, and accident) during the long days of sailing and long hours of trekking made me tense, but this was eased by the sweet and welcoming people whose paths I crossed randomly. The moments I had in all your regions were my happiest.

But Afro, O my Sweet Afro, don't you know that the trees are falling?

I will constantly remind you of your grace, Afro. You are grand and magnificent! I will constantly remind you of your beauty, strength, and power. Maybe this will awaken your youth and encourage your adults to become united once again. Maybe this will inspire them to be the righteous and selfless leaders who will maximally utilize the resources you possess, not for selfish benefits but for your growth and advancement to become the world's ruling nation.

But Afro, O my Sweet Afro, why are your people suffering despite your proven strength, wealth, and power? Haven't you realized, dear Afro, that you are suffering from yet another act of colonization?

The feckless "democratic" rulers of your land, although indigenous, have a shady act, cunningly violating the laws that ensure justice and peace. The dubious politicians are desperate to attain power; they want to accomplish their selfish ambitions. Corruption has become minister of state affairs, Oppression is now the speaker of the House of Commons, and Anguish is the reward for anyone who dares to question their ways. They engrave bitterness in the hearts of others.

Dear Afro, can these be called a betrayal from your own kinsmen?

Factionism, favoritism, selfishness, greed are what you experience from the ne'er-do-well democratic rulers selected to coordinate. Terrorism and pressurization are what you get when you try to voice your opinion as regards coordination or correcting the leaders' wrong choices.

Isn't this yet another act of slavery at its peak? Sweet Afro, isn't this yet another betrayal?

Many are homeless, but a politician has countless huge mansions. The magnate lives off the pawns; the unqualified children of powerful men get the job while the qualified talented poor graduate is left unemployed. Many are penniless beggars, but the greedy leaders possess billions of dollars in funds comfortably seated in the banks of Western countries through illegal financial outflow.

Irrespective of Westerners' cruel exploitation and colonization, I strongly believe the amply blessed and powerful Afro I know and I've experienced ought to have healed the damage done to her to some greater extent.

There's still much liberation to be done, dear Afro. Not just for technology, infrastructure, education, or well-equipped health care. But into a world of justice and accountability, where there are incorruptible, unapologetically loyal, honest, and selfless rulers. The kind of leader I am determined to be! The leader who leads the change!

I will understand my role to serve and serve diligently, be passionate about the welfare of my people, be zealous about the growth and development of my land.

Oh Afro. This is a call to awake! This is the challenge!

You are a visioneer with dreams and determination who longs to illuminate her world and make it a great place to be, who desires the growth of her nation, who thirsts for an evolved world beyond the infinite innovation, unending expansion of research and development.

A world free of corrupt, discriminatory, egocentric, selfish, and covetous leaders.

A world of love, joy, abundance, comfort, kindness, harmony, unquantified goodness.

A world of distinction, improvement, development, and innovations.

I will remind you that you are intelligent, smart, strong, and very powerful!

Remember how united, problem-solving, goal-oriented, loving, and kind you used to be with your fellow humans? Those acts won victories against the invaders. I will remind you to exhibit these traits again.

Against all odds, you will become great again!

True leaders will emerge to lead the change, corruption will fail, and democracy will rule!

Your wealth will be distributed evenly, and your economy will lead!

The nation is becoming a brighter place to live!

GROWING TOGETHER

BREAKING CYCLES OF TRAUMA

Dr. Samniqueka Halsey

"Are you okay?" Christopher asks me, pulling me from my daydreaming.

"Yeah, I'm good," I say, sitting on my apartment patio, sipping my pre-workout supplement drink. I'm in my favorite chair, a papasan with a large comfy pillow. This time is the first in a while that I've been able to sit and not think about anything. I listen to the wind blowing, the trees rustling, and glimpse the occasional flying bird. I purposely chose an apartment on the outskirts of town, a little bit closer to nature.

"Okay, just checking," he says, pulling his chair closer to me. I love how he checks up on me. He knows that sometimes I get inside my head too much about work, and this weekend I'm unplugging from my normal day-to-day routine. Although I'm a tenure-track professor, a computational ecologist studying tick-borne diseases, I try to maintain a decent work-life balance. The semester might be over, but there is plenty to worry about with my students in the field, trapping deer mice and prairie voles to determine how restoration efforts affect tick abundance. It's my birthday weekend, and I'm determined to take four days off to spend with my partner.

I let my graduate students know they are to contact me only for emergencies until I return. Per my therapist's suggestion, I also set up an out-of-office email message for the first time during my two-year term as an assistant professor. Of course, unplugging is a rare commodity. Every day, I can feel the weight of the world on my shoulders and often feel guilty about taking time off. There's always something that needs to be done: a paper to write, a grant to submit. But as they say, save yourself first. So I am continuing to find ways to practice self-care, and sometimes that might just mean unplugging from the world and escaping into my little bubble for a few days.

It's an official #StayAtHomeBaeCation, a change from my usual birthday celebrations spent at somebody's beach, as we are in the middle of a worldwide pandemic that has not shown any sign of relenting due to slow vaccination rates and increased emergence of variants.

"I'm trying to stay in the present," I tell Christopher once he sits down. He knows it's one of my coping strategies to keep my mind from racing. Breathe in. Breathe out. Listen to the environment. Use all five senses to focus on what's right in front of you.

It's been a while since Christopher and I have spent time together. We are in a long-distance relationship, and considering that the world has been in a pandemic for the last fourteen months, traveling has been difficult. Communication is strained at times, but we are trying to make it work. So I want to enjoy this. I want to enjoy him. Cooking, watching movies, and spending time at the community pool soaking up a bit of sun.

"Ready to go to the gym?" he asks.

"Yup, just waiting on you." I laugh and take another sip of my drink.

It doesn't take long for us to walk to my apartment's fully equipped gym. When searching for an apartment after accepting my job, I took one look at the gym, two pools, and hot tub and asked the leasing agent for the contract to sign.

Exercise is part of my self-care regime, spending a couple hours a day focused on aligning mind and body. Honestly, anything that gets me up and moving energizes me, whether it's hiking, biking, or just exploring the world around me in general. It wasn't until adulthood that I fully realized these interests, and I consider myself lucky that my academic career overlaps with my interests in outdoor exploration. Each year, for example, I visit the beaches of the Great Lakes to monitor the sand dunes that provide protection from high waves, reducing coastal flooding and damage. It doesn't take long for me to complete my work, finding, measuring, and recording each individual Pitcher's thistle (*Cirsium pitcheri*), a plant species threatened by habitat fragmentation and degradation. Once I finish, I can then partake of the sun and water, returning to my self-care regime.

As Christopher opens the door to the gym, my phone buzzes.

"Thank you," I say as I enter, pulling my phone from my pocket to check the message.

It's a purple-haired Bitmoji image from one of my undergraduate mentees, Tina, with the words "Knock Knock."

"Hey, how's Costa Rica?" I text back as I go to the stationary bike to warm up. Tina is currently out of the country for a research experience for undergraduates (REU), studying the mating behaviors of the ground anole, a small lizard found in the rainforests there.

"It's going pretty OK," she replies. "I just had a meeting with Ty to talk about alternatives to working with Kara while here. Our relationship hasn't been so great. Other than that, I'm having an amazing time."

My heart drops. Tina always tries to look on the bright side of things and was so excited about this trip. She had applied to several REU programs, hoping to be able to go somewhere new and conduct field research during her last summer of college. The pandemic had caused many program cancellations, especially study abroad programs. When faced with the decision of whether to accept a US-based program, Tina had been offered a last-minute opportunity to go abroad with Kara, a second-year postdoctoral fellow in biological sciences who had obtained special travel permission to conduct research in Costa Rica during the pandemic. Although a natural resources major, Tina had worked with several professors in the biology department since her interests in animal behavior aligned more closely with those faculty, and she had met Kara through that department.

Now it sounds like everything is falling apart. Tina is on the other side of the world, in a foreign country where she does not speak the language. I need to know more and try to help her through this . . . less than five minutes into my warm-up. Despite my veins teeming with the caffeine equivalent of two cups of coffee delivered by my pre-workout drink, and my anticipation of spending time with Christopher in the gym as we feed off each other's energy to #GoHard, #BeastMode, this constitutes an emergency. So I go out into the lobby and call Tina.

Tina's time in Costa Rica reminds me of my experience as an undergraduate student ten years earlier. I had obtained what I thought was the opportunity of a lifetime: my first summer field assistantship, trapping prairie dogs in the Four Corners states (Colorado, Arizona, New Mexico, and Utah). I had applied for the position with a fellow classmate, Chaya. Although we had different backgrounds—Chaya is of Indian origin, whereas my ancestors were the Balanta and Temne people from Guinea-Bissau and Sierra Leone in West Africa, via the transatlantic slave trade—we had worked well together in our ecology class.

Chaya and I were both anxious about the job, checking in with each other to see if either of us had heard back, wondering if we would both be hired and able to work together again. A week before the position started, we found out that we both had gotten the job. Road trip!

I had my list: Sleeping bag. Tent. Camp stove. Hiking boots. Field clothes. I was excited.

Similarly, Tina had to figure out what she needed to leave for Costa Rica: Passport. Field clothes. Hiking boots. Camera. Tina was excited.

We drove Chaya's truck from Chicago to Colorado to meet our team. Driving through the Rocky Mountains was amazing. We watched the aspen trees go by, saw bighorn sheep traipse across cliffs, and played in snow in the middle of May—all of it a far different experience from growing up in Detroit.

In hindsight, I know that I made some mistakes during those first few weeks in the field. And I also know I was not given grace or the benefit of the doubt by my peers and supervisors.

Back then, nature was all new to me. I was timid, hesitant, and sometimes afraid. And on occasion, I'd complain about the heat, the sweat, and the physical exertion.

Nonetheless, I participated in every activity.

I quickly learned to camp, as campsites were our sole accommodations. It didn't take long for camping to give me a sense of joy, a feeling that I have since passed along to my nieces and nephews through yearly camping trips. My older cousin bought and sent me a tent for that field assistantship, and now I have four of various sizes to accommodate my niblings.

In our downtime, I joined the team in hiking in the surrounding forests, climbing rocks, and pushing my body past limits I had never needed to cross. On the first hike I took that summer, I thought the same thing as my three-year-old nephew when I took him hiking for the first time; he told me it smelled like vegetables. I have a passion for hiking now that I did not have as a kid growing up in the city.

I also had the opportunity to explore the South Rim of the Grand Canyon. In school, I learned how it was carved by the Colorado River, but to see it in person brought into perspective its vastness. Due to my fear of heights, I took my time as I descended a few miles down. Unbeknownst to me, with each and every step I collected blisters. Because I had not purchased actual hiking boots, but Timberlands.

However, this was just the beginning of my hiking journey. In the years to come, I would, with a proper pair of Vasque hiking boots, roam the hills of Ireland and eventually hike Mount Olympus in Greece.

I was similarly awestruck on a trip to Petrified Forest National Park. Being able to walk around the semi-desert shrub steppe and examine fossilized wood felt surreal. Totally different from observing museum specimens. To stand in the same location as those fallen trees from hundreds of millions of years ago showcased the everlasting endurance of nature.

I thought I would share this adventure and experience with Chaya, but I didn't. There were six field assistants hired for the summer, and after a week of training, we were split into teams of three. Chaya and I were on separate teams, assigned to different study sites.

I soon felt alone and isolated. I was the only Black person. It soon became apparent that I was also the poorest. Nightly hangouts at bars and restaurants were not in my budget. So I stayed at the campsite eating the noodles I cooked on my camp stove. It did not take long for me to be labeled as antisocial.

In fact, the other team members spoke privately with the graduate student in charge of the project, who then decided to send me home. Without conversation, less than a month into the position that was supposed to last four months, I was given a bus ticket home. Imagine traveling to a location in a truck with plenty of space and then leaving on a Greyhound. I couldn't carry all of the belongings I'd brought with me, so I had to throw away several items including a camp stove and food.

I distinctly remember the graduate student telling me, "I don't know what's going on and I don't have time to figure it out. You seem to be the problem, so I'm sending you home. I just need my research completed."

Now I listen to Tina tell me about her experience. She is the only Black student. She's sleep deprived and doesn't feel safe. And Kara is not listening or understanding, only concerned about collecting research data.

I ask Tina what she wants and assure her that we will figure it out. If she decides to come back, I will help her find another research opportunity. But Tina wants to stick it out. She doesn't want to quit, she just wants to be treated fairly. She wants the experience that was described when the project was presented to her—monitoring anole mating patterns and having a bit of downtime to explore the beautiful country. Tina is determined to try to make the best of her situation and worries that this is a reflection on her. That she can't cut it.

When I was in a similar position, I did not have anyone to talk to. No one who could reassure me that I wasn't the problem. I decide to be that someone for Tina.

The rest of the day for me goes on as usual, though Tina remains on my mind. How can I help her? I watch Netflix and enjoy rich red velvet cupcakes from a local bakery as I think about who I can connect Tina with should she decide to come home early.

As I sit on my couch eating double chocolate gelato, I also debate whether I should send an email to Kara or even her supervisor.

In the midst of this, I receive another text.

Tina is being sent home. A plane ticket has already been bought. She is forced to take a six-hour car ride to an airport where no one speaks English and go through customs in a foreign country alone. She's told she needs too many accommodations, and it's getting in the way of Kara's research.

I try to encourage Tina, even though my mood is soured. I wonder if Tina is crying during the car ride in the same way I cried on the bus. I wonder if my assurances that this is not her fault outweigh the doubts being sown by a supposed mentor.

I am crying. My anxiety spikes. *Will anything ever change?*

Despite initiatives aimed at increasing diversity in STEM, researchers are still putting their research and data before the health and safety of students. They are not respecting and understanding cultural differences and experiences. A postdoc who has been doing research for years and is used to long days and lack of sleep cannot expect the same of someone who has been doing it for only three weeks. Adjustments should have been made and communicated, especially when Kara found the workload increased due to a reduction in team size. And she definitely shouldn't have been exploiting undergraduate students by overworking them and not giving them time off.

The timing of everything is terrible. I'm now depressed and overwhelmed with anxiety. Christopher checks in on me.

I check in on Tina as she travels back to the States through inclement weather and flight delays, because I know how it feels. Every step of the way, I make sure she knows I'm there as I wish I'd had someone to check in on me.

It is an honor that Tina trusts me enough to have her back. I can only hope my support every step of the way makes her path a bit easier so she can not only achieve her goal of pursuing a PhD but also thrive in the never-ending struggle as a woman of color in academia. It takes only a small act of compassion and understanding to break the cycles of trauma that cause harm to minoritized students who decide to embark on a lifelong academic journey. Cycles of trauma caused by a system that demands tolerance of unjust harm and egregious self-sacrifice to succeed, no matter the physical and mental toll it takes.

I see a lot of myself in Tina and still struggle with the cultural and class differences of my chosen career path and upbringing. Undeterred, through therapy I work to achieve a balance between my work and personal life, including finding new ways to practice self-care. In addition to setting boundaries and reserving time for myself, I make a concerted effort to give and receive grace, not only with my students and colleagues but also those in my personal life with whom I develop emotional connections.

While this weekend has been an emotional rollercoaster, I consider it an attestation that I can achieve a work–personal life balance that feels natural to me. I am able to finish the weekend by enjoying my time spent with Christopher, ready to return to work and connect Tina with a colleague surveying grassland birds at Illinois's Midewin National Tallgrass Prairie.

BLACK WOMEN IN NATURE, BLACK WOMEN AND NATURE

Joelle K. Jenkins

Black women in nature,
we came to create,
and there's nothing greater.
One could say it's innate.
Moving like goddesses,
with our hair emulating tree canopies,
melanin holding the richness of Earth,
and an aura mirroring nature's versatility.

Black women and nature,
a combination that nourishes the mind, body, and soul,
a powerful essence more valuable than gold.
Nature gives us the autonomy we need

to sustain ourselves, to help us succeed.
Farming, hunting, gardening, and more,
woven into our historical fabric,
a crucial part of our timeline that will not be ignored.

Black women in nature,
the (re)birth of a movement.
Rightfully reclaiming our space,
a much-needed improvement.
We are unstoppable,
for the storms we endure just make our roots stronger.
As much as others deny it,
we are essential, like water.

Black women and nature,
a coexistence that speaks our truth,
bringing peace and healing to our communities
through and through.
And there's no need to prove ourselves;
the evidence is apparent.
Undoubtedly influencing everything we touch,
do you feel us, omnipresent?

ZION TRAIN

Kelly GreenLight Thomas

Jah free the people
Over hills and valleys too
—Buju Banton

This is for children of the soil. First- and second-generation immigrants with souls from black and brown places covered in green, brought up in cities with island hearts. Those who long for stretches of horizon over seas they have never seen. Imports and exports traversing story. knowing. place. We have come and gone by choice by force by air by water by fire searching everywhere for a home we know is out there . . . somewhere.

My love affair with nature began indoors listening to the deep, bassy sounds of roots reggae. This politically and socially conscious music that collided with me at about age ten was full of references to mystic mountains, verdant promised lands, and fresh vegetables (nods to Tony Rebel). The songs were also full of homophobic and misogynistic messages, which, thankfully, did not take root in me as much as those of freedom, collectivism, and black pride.

Reggae presented the outdoors to me as a place to commune with god in myself, a much-needed relief growing up as a conflicted Catholic teen. I was enamored with the undercurrent of mysticism and liberation found in nature that wound through the trance-evoking melodies. Regular listening cultivated in me an internal rhythm, an external resoluteness, and a lasting vision of a tangible freedom constructed outside of my conservative reality. Sizzla chanting on "Solid as a Rock" conjured within me an elemental strength that would resonate for years to come as I trekked through this or that forest, trailed by a line of other black and brown freedom lovers. At this moment in 2022, I'm proud to say that I have cultivated such liberation lines in Germany, Dominica, Brazil, Haiti, and throughout the US.

Reminiscing on sojourns through various homelands of the African diaspora, I take a deeper breath. My heart swells at the memory of the hush on the trail, the wide eyes of those who are waking up for the first time, and the shared humility in **feeling** our place among the lavish wildness of creation. Oh, us children of the diaspora have seen so much and have felt even more than we have seen. From the bridge between worlds that I grew up on, I feel most at home with the rocks, trees, oceans, and open sky, face to the sun or moon. The reggae griots knew all along what sense of belonging and purpose was to be found in the natural world. Time and again, I've seen the faces of my chosen siblings soften and brighten during an outdoor expedition. It is the stuff that freedom songs are made of.

I've been leading outdoor experiences specifically for black folks since 2013, when I hosted my first Black Arts Retreat. Black Arts Retreat, or BAR, is a community arts organization I founded some years after attending a very beautiful—but very white and faraway—arts retreat down south.

My experience in the rolling mountains of Asheville, North Carolina, gave me the motivation to collect my own group of artists that looked and felt more like me. I wanted to experience creative immersion with other young black and brown nature-loving city dwellers. Those who were ready to explore beyond the cement blocks we were prescribed. I was born and raised in New Jersey, "the Garden State," but at the time, I had seen very few of our gardens. The retreat, set for the greener side of New Jersey, would change all that. The prospect of adding a cadre of creative folk to the mix was a dream come true.

Just a couple of hours outside of our concrete jungles were the teeming forest reserves of the Delaware Water Gap. I had never actually been camping, but back then, I was a leap-first type of person. Thankfully, my partner at the time had some experience in the great outdoors and later, a community elder also agreed to help us rough it. So, in the full audacity of my early twenties, I gathered nineteen people for a camping retreat, including a man over sixty and a new mother with her infant.

Despite my being brand-new to hosting outdoor events, much less a retreat, the preparation all went smoothly. I had already been teaching and preparing creative lessons for others for some years at that point, and my skill sets carried over well. Not being a driver myself, I knew that the issue of transportation could be a barrier to accessing the wilder outdoor spaces. That being the case, we arranged carpools for everyone and planned to drive down together.

The morning of the retreat, the eldest among us, Brother Farrad, showed up first, fully decked in olive outdoor gear and hiking boots. His truck was efficiently packed with a New York apartment–sized tent, cook stove, gas can, and assortment of camping doodads I couldn't identify at the time. Every summer, Brother Farrad spent his time taking the young men of his church out to the woods for overnight adventures, so he was more than prepared for a journey such as ours. I had gotten connected to him through Mia X, a powerhouse poet in the Newark arts scene who was to lead the spoken word workshop for the retreat. It was our first time meeting, but Brother Farrad's warm and cheerful demeanor made conversation easy while we waited for the others to arrive. Most showed up one by one, except for the new mother and her baby and the set of brothers who could almost be twins but weren't.

Our meetup spot was the parking lot next to Mia's apartment complex in Newark, the most central location for everyone coming from the surrounding cities. There were musicians, rappers, and actors from around North Jersey and writers, painters, and fashion designers from NYC, each showing up with their own music and flavor for the collective pot. We brought so much life to the parking lot that day. Even the pavement was glad to witness our opening circle of breath and drum and sage along with any passersby or neighbors gazing out of their windows at the colorful sight. Giddy conversation followed the ceremony as we piled into the biggest cars and vans. We arrived on-site a bit later than expected and set up camp with only a healthy amount of confusion. Then, to my horror, the moment the last tent was staked and zipped, the sky opened up and poured rain on our tent village.

I could have cried. Gasps and yelps went up from retreaters as they dashed to take cover in their tents. Brother Farrad, Mia, Purple (my camping enthusiast partner), my sister Tracee (our resident yogi), and I made a soggy round to help folks patch leaks. I thought everything was ruined, but what happened next is the stuff BAR lore is made of. It became clear that the rain was staying the night and our outdoor agenda was thwarted, but there at the center of our tent village was the tent mansion Brother Farrad had brought along. With no phone service and nowhere to go, we ended up sitting all together in that huge tent with a whole new plan. We had a laugh at the irony of it all and then sang songs and told stories until late into the night. Most memorably, we played a storytelling game where each person added a line to a tale about a misunderstood swamp monster. In our telling, the creature had emerged from its murky cave not to terrify but to teach our hero a lesson, as shadows often do. The bright eyes and deep belly laughs from that damp night remind me now just how much joy can come from a perceived mess. I thought for sure folks would leave or want their money back, but instead they embraced it all as part of the adventure.

The next morning was crisp but sunny as folks huddled around our fire under blankets, chuckling about how fun and random our night had been. Then a friend brought out her flute and between melodies began sharing the Indigenous history of the land we were camping on (respect and gratitude to the Lenape people). We never got around to yoga, but our crafting and poetry workshop followed the fireside cipher. In the workshop, we fashioned headdresses and other adornment from ribbon and scrap fabric while pondering place and purpose amid the enchanting fall foliage. We all appreciated the time to write and reflect after our dramatic break from the ordinary. Even though almost nothing went according to plan, everyone agreed that being together in the spirit of creative play had been more than enough and just what was needed.

Later, at a nearby river, one retreater caught me by surprise, talking about, "I can just see us at the tenth annual Black Arts Retreat." I smiled and laughed with her, but my bewildered mind said, You **can**?! I had only thought of making it safely through that one night. I had no concept of what our embrace of the chaos had set in motion.

At Black Arts Retreat, we describe ourselves as "a home for black genius: providing restorative experiences that connect participants to art, whole wellness, nature, themselves, and each other." Our mission grew directly out of that rainy night at the Delaware Water Gap. The year 2023 marks ten years since that spontaneity, creativity, and collective agreement to "go with it" started something that has now touched four continents and people all over the globe.

I look back and thank the rain. That rain, that mud, those clouds, the river next to our camp, the surrounding trees. They held us that night, through to the next morning's fire and oatmeal, where our sister played the flute to honor the original people of the land, and another conjured some improvisational poetry. It was indeed a vision of Zion (nods to Garnett Silk). In reggae and Rastafari, Zion is the promised land, a place of unity, peace, and freedom. This was our glimpse of what liberation can look like: our rhythm dictated by the elements around us, living in surrender and story and communion.

The soil has kept a record of the suppressed histories of our ancestors, and I have felt a haunting sadness, grief, and fear on the trails and in the campgrounds of the US. Then there's the range of casual violence to endure out there, from scrutinizing looks to gazes that purposely edit me out of the view, quite contrary to the feeling of steady belonging I experience with the rocks and mosses. Thankfully, nature is not neutral. It is—she is—decidedly loving, generous, and inviting, without judgment or discrimination. In taking on the outdoors together and facing the social dynamics imposed therein, the Black Arts Retreat community supports each other through inherited fears and makes strides toward healing from the harmful experiences. The trees have been our witness.

Over the years, we have come to know—retreat after retreat, hike after hike, barbecue after barbecue—that our promised land, our Zion, isn't bound to any particular time or topography but rather is something that can be created anywhere we are present and connected to the fullness of nature in, as, and around our own selves.

JUST LIKE ME

Sharon Dorsey

It's the middle of the week on a hot summer day, and the smell of animal feces is rank. Camille and her classmates are reaching their respective olfactory thresholds as they complete their final task for the workday.

"God! I'm so sick of cleaning poop all day! Is this really what it takes to impress vet schools?" her classmate Tracy exclaims.

"You're telling me!" Jessica follows. "My parents made me take this job to prove I could take care of a new dog."

This isn't even that bad compared to the constant stench wafting from my brothers' room, Camille muses, using her forearm to brush strands of hair out of her face. "At least this is the last thing we have to do for the day. Plus, Mr. Jacobs said he had some exciting news to share with us about tomorrow. I think we're getting a new addition to our center!"

For the past four weeks, the three high schoolers have been volunteering at Jefferson County Wildlife Rehabilitation Center. The rehab center is situated in a cozy residential area in Brooklyn. Concerned residents and motorists frequently shuttle in injured American robins, eastern cottontails, and box turtles, hoping they can be nursed back to health. Over the years, the staff of five has always been stretched thin, so seasonal volunteers are expected to do the bulk of the dirty work during the busiest part of the year.

Camille doubts vet school is in the cards for her with how expensive tuition is but has enjoyed being around wildlife and her friends' pets for as long as she can remember. She aspires to have a successful life working with animals but can't imagine how those two goals are compatible without significant debt, so she accepts that dirty work and menial pay is just part of working in the wildlife field.

In contrast, Camille's classmates, Tracy and Jessica, can all but claim their spot at the top veterinary school based on their parents' bank accounts. So this dirty work is certainly not what they expected to be doing all summer. Tracy's and Jessica's privileges always baffle Camille, who was told from an early age that she could not always get what she wanted and to expect to make concessions when it came to what she wished she had.

"Hey, Camille," Tracy begins as the final kennel is being cleaned, "I know it's my turn on the schedule to hose down these sponges, but could you do me a favor and wash them today? This smell is literally making me nauseated."

"Oh. Erm . . . I guess I can," Camille responds, annoyed. Why didn't I just say no? It's not like she would have done me the favor if I had asked. She's going to start taking advantage of my kindness if I'm not careful. Maybe I should say something . . .

Before Camille can say anything else, Tracy drops her bucket and exits the room, her blonde ponytail swaying from side to side. Camille and Jessica are left to pack up the cleaning supplies and return the various critters to their freshly sanitized spaces. Camille closes the door on a cage now holding a squirrel with a bandaged tail when Mr. Jacobs, the center's supervisor, pops his head in the human-sized door frame.

"I can never get enough of that clean smell!" he says, grinning. "Thanks, ladies! Care to join us for the staff meeting?"

A few minutes later, the handful of rehab center staff members gather in front of Mr. Jacobs in the back break room. He is a middle-aged man but has a spunky youthfulness about him. Some of his chestnut brown hair brushes over his eyebrows as he speaks animatedly during the daily announcements.

"Lastly, the news you've all been waiting for! Tomorrow, we have a very important guest visiting us—the newly appointed commissioner of the Department of Environmental Conservation, Commissioner Daniel Thompson."

Mr. Jacobs looks awkwardly in the direction of Tracy, Jessica, and Camille. "I want you three to be on your best behavior and do your best to look presentable. Camille, maybe wear the hat I issued you to . . . you know . . . tame your hair a bit," he continues, shifting his gaze to anywhere in the room but her direction.

Camille's S-shaped, 4A curls are loosely restrained with a triangular folded bandana tied around her head, about two inches back from her forehead. A sea of coils, some combed and some tangled together, is hanging freely behind her head. Predictably, the bandana has moved throughout the day, freeing several stray hairs and shooting noticeable frizz in multiple directions from her crown. Jeez, it's also not like I had much of a chance to look in the mirror and brush my hair today!

"Yes, sir," she says quietly. She stops breathing the moment she feels the eyes of all her coworkers shift in her direction, as they realize how different she is from the rest of the group.

"See everyone here at nine o'clock sharp tomorrow!" Mr. Jacobs says nonchalantly and dismisses the group for the day.

As Camille walks in the front door of her family's townhouse, the smell of steamed shrimp fills her nostrils. Mom must have had one of her better days at work, Camille thinks to herself, instantly feeling much more at home in more ways than one. On bad days, her mother is liable to throw her hands up and make a microwaved dinner.

"Cameron! Corey! Come make the table!" Camille's mother shouts to her sons, her head aimed up to the kitchen ceiling. "Oh! Welcome home, baby! I made your favorite: shrimp and grits."

Camille's momentary bliss is immediately ruined by her older brothers' tall and lanky bodies thumping down the stairs and tussling the top of her head. "Hey, weirdo! Finally make any **human** friends today?" Cameron says.

Since their tweens, they would pick on her for being more interested in animals than normal girl things. The boys played basketball with neighborhood kids at the local park while Camille sat alone on the bench and fed squirrels.

"No," Camille says, making a face. "But a little birdie told me you **still** haven't worked up the nerve to ask Chelsea out on a date."

"Now stop it, you two!" their mom interjects as she turns from the stove. "Cameron, stop picking on your sister and grab that sweet tea from the fridge for me. Dinner's just about ready."

The four of them sit around the table, and each recounts their day. Their mom **did** have a good day at work: she shares that after five years in her position as an administrative assistant at a local physician's office, she is up for a promotion. Her brothers each give animated accounts of their workdays as well. Camille is the last to share.

"And how was your day, honey?" her mother kindly inquires.

Two years ago, Camille's ninth grade biology class had been given a presentation by a zookeeper about how she came into the profession and what her job responsibilities were. A lightbulb had been turned on inside Camille: she wanted to pursue that career too! She had arrived at school the next day with cut-out photos of wildlife to decorate her locker with, which caught the eye of her classmate James.

"What's this? You tryna be the next Jane Goodall?" James had asked harshly. "Because only white people have enough free time to play in the jungle. Who cares about monkeys when our people got bigger problems in our own neighborhoods!"

Camille was so taken aback she didn't know what to say. Her dreams of working with wildlife had just been dismissed as an unrealistic and unimportant career. Ever since that day, she had kept her passions more tempered and rarely talked to others, including her family, about her interest in wildlife conservation. Her decision to work at the rehabilitation center was a big step for her, but she didn't widely broadcast her activities at the center to others.

Camille looks across the dinner table at her brothers, who had checked out of the conversation, leaning shoulder-to-shoulder watching a TikTok on Corey's phone. "Same old, same old," she responds dishearteningly.

After dinner, Camille and her brothers complete their assigned cleanup chores. Camille retires to the privacy of her bedroom and sits at her vanity facing the attached mirror. Her hair looks even more disheveled than at work, thanks to her brother. Camille decides she will wear a hat tomorrow to cover her wild hair. She will not take the chance of having a bad hair day in front of the commissioner.

Is it really so bad to want to work with plants and animals? Camille ponders as she twists her hair for bed. *Not everyone can fight the big fights like homelessness . . . and poverty . . . and police brutality. Caring for nature and wildlife can still be impactful, right? . . . Or maybe it is just for white people. All the educators and caregivers at the zoo and aquarium I've seen have been white, and the only wildlife biologists I can name are Steve Irwin, Jeff Corwin, and Jane Goodall.*

As her mind grows weary from her internal quandary, she crawls into bed and falls asleep watching the collage of cutouts from *Zoobooks* magazine hung on the adjacent wall.

"Everyone, I'd like to introduce you to Dr. Daniel Thompson, the commissioner of the Department of Environmental Conservation," Mr. Jacobs announces in the break room the next morning. "Folks, introduce yourselves."

Standing beside Mr. Jacobs is a broad man in his mid-forties, towering at six and a half feet tall, with coffee-colored skin, long locs neatly tied behind his head, and a wide smile on his face. *Wait . . . Is this really the commissioner for the entire DEC?! He's Black!*

"Erm . . . Camille?" Mr. Jacobs breaks her trance.

"Oh. Sorry. Hi. I'm Camille Jenkins. I'm also a junior at Eastern Technical High School." *And somebody needs to pinch me because I don't believe what I'm seeing.*

"Well, it's very nice to meet you all," Commissioner Thompson says in a deep, calming voice. "I was hoping one of you could give me a quick tour of your facility. Do you mind, Camille?"

"Sure!" *Oh my God!* I have so many questions to ask him.

The rest of the staff saunters off for a typical day as Camille leads Commissioner Thompson outside, toward the avian building.

"So, Mr. Jacobs hasn't told me that much about you," Commissioner Thompson begins. "Can I ask what made you want to work with animals here at the rehab center?"

Camille begins excitedly, "Well, on my walk home from middle school every day, I'd usually see finches and crows eating food scraps on the side of Clarkson Street, but then the cars zoomed by and startled them. Oh! And the sight of roadkill just makes me so sad. I **always** see an opossum carcass when I'm walking down Melrose Avenue, and I just wish people would be more careful and watch out for them, you know? Like the possum is just trying to live its life and didn't do anything to deserve getting hit!"

Camille's thoughts flood out to the commissioner as the dam she's pieced together over the years breaks. She is filled with nervousness and eagerness—she is speaking to someone she never thought could exist. *Is it possible that he also likes animals as much as I do?* I wonder, *is he going to think I'm a weirdo too?*

"Yeah, that area **is** pretty highly trafficked and, with Providence Park so close by, it makes for good foraging grounds for the opossum. Those urban wildlife species are definitely in a predicament coming to more populated areas to find food."

"Wait! You know Providence Park? Did you pass it on your way here?"

Commissioner Thompson lets out a short chuckle. "Something like that! I've passed it a lot considering I was born and raised in Jefferson Heights." Jefferson Heights! That's the neighborhood just next to mine!

"Seriously?! Wow!" Camille exclaims. *What a coincidence!*

They continue to talk throughout the rest of the tour. Camille leads him through the different buildings, but instead of telling him about the facility, she is asking more questions. She learns that Commissioner Thompson was an athlete like her brothers but left Brooklyn to attend the University of Georgia, where he played football and studied fisheries and wildlife sciences. He later earned a PhD from Texas A&M University, where he met his wife. The two of them bounced around various states and then settled back in New York so he could accept the commissioner position.

Camille is learning so much about the commissioner, but she hasn't worked up the courage to ask what she really wants to know. They return to the main building of the center with a pause in the conversation that must be a little too long, because she feels her nerves rearing up again. I guess now is as good a time as any.

"Commissioner Thompson, can I ask you a question?"

Sensing her seriousness, he nods and gestures to sit on the bench beside the walkway to the main lobby.

Camille takes a deep breath. She speaks her mind about the apprehension she's had surrounding pursuing her interest in wildlife conservation: how she often feels othered in positions like this with wildlife work, how she'd previously believed it wasn't a realistic career path for a Black person, and how she had never met or heard of a Black biologist or environmental scientist, which contributed to her continued belief that Black folk just didn't work in wildlife fields.

"So I guess I was just wondering what made **you** want to work with animals and what your experience has been like, navigating this field . . . you know . . . as a Black man?"

Commissioner Thompson's smile grows larger than ever.

"Well, well . . . so that's what's really been going through that head of yours," the commissioner begins. "I'm sorry to tell you that there's not enough time right now to share my journey with you in its entirety. But I do have three things I can share with you now. First, I view my job as a way to fight systemic racism, which denies people like us the opportunity to make meaningful contributions to conservation. In this role, I work to break down barriers so Black people can have a say in policies impacting wildlife in their communities.

"Second, you're not taught about them in school, but Black wildlife biologists do exist. Start by looking up a friend and mentor of mine, Ms. Sheila Minor Huff. She's a retired wildlife biologist from Washington, DC, who faced discrimination, but her resiliency and persistence paved the way for folks like us in this field. Unfortunately, that feeling of being othered and experiencing microaggressions won't go away, but it's important to know whose shoulders we're standing on and to form a community with other brothers and sisters doing this work, which I'd love to do for you.

"Which leads me to my last point. What would you say to continuing this conversation upstate, at our headquarters? We have an urban wildlife policy internship underway this summer that is based out of our office in Albany. We have a few spots left, and I will personally recommend you."

"Commissioner Thompson, I really appreciate you taking the time to talk to me about this," Camille responds fervently. "You've opened my eyes to so much and I'd love to take the internship and learn even more from you!"

"Of course. Here, take my business card and talk it over with your folks. If you decide to join us, I'll square things away with Mr. Jacobs about transferring your position from here," Commissioner Thompson says, pulling out a card from his wallet. "And let me reiterate this: if you need anything from me—big or small—just give me a call, alright? I'd be happy to support you on your journey in any way I can." Commissioner Thompson offers his hand and the two shake before he returns to his car. Camille returns to the bench and takes a moment to reflect on their meeting.

Wow . . . this is exactly what I needed to hear. Who knew there have been Black wildlife biologists for decades? Ms. Sheila Minor Huff is such a trailblazer; I'd love to follow her path of paving the way for more folks like me to pursue this career. Maybe I can do this. . . . No. I **know** *I want to do this! Dr. Camille Jenkins, wildlife biologist, does have a nice ring to it after all!*

Note: Camille's experience is based on the author's own story of finding inspiration to pursue her dream of working in wildlife conservation.

Follow her journey on her social media pages: @SharInNature on Twitter and Instagram. Dr. Thompson's character is loosely based on Jerome Ford, assistant director of the US Fish and Wildlife Service's Migratory Bird Program. Read more about him at www.audubon.org/news/getting-know-jerome-ford-governments-top-bird-official. Dr. Sheila Minor Huff is a real-life Black female researcher whose story can be read at www.nytimes.com/2018/03/19/us/twitter-mystery-photo.html.

THE (UN)WRITTEN RULEBOOK

Jasmin Graham

I grew up in South Carolina and come from a long line of fishers. My fondest memories are of fishing with my dad, eating fresh-caught seafood at my Grandma Evelina's house, and telling stories around the dinner table. These experiences and my deep coastal roots in Myrtle Beach, South Carolina, instilled in me a love of the ocean and motivated my work as a marine scientist who specializes in sharks and rays. I'm the first person to receive a science degree in my family; although members of my family have been using the scientific method and studying fish for generations, we just never called it science. My grandmother was an expert fisher, and to be that good, you must have a deep understanding of fish behavior and ecology.

In recent years, the plight of Black people in their attempts to simply **be** in various spaces has received increased national attention. As the Black Lives Matter movement became more mainstream, we saw more and more folks with signs, bumper stickers, and email signatures showing their support for the movement. Cases of overt racism gained more media exposure. Each of these incidents has rightly sparked outrage across the United States, but these are only the stories that make it to the news. One of the more recent and heavily televised examples was the incident of Christian Cooper, a Black birder, being berated by a white woman in Central Park. The viral video began a cascade of events that led me to found an organization with three other Black women: Minorities in Shark Sciences (MISS).

Black scientists face the same issues as the rest of the Black community, though in unique contexts. We go into natural spaces in the name of science to collect data, and we travel globally to attend conferences and present our research. We go into these spaces knowing lynchings and sundown towns are not a thing of the past, despite what many think. There are many spaces and places where Black people, of any occupation or expertise, are not welcome and are not safe. As Black scientists venture through worlds, we assess and reassess our personal safety in ways our non-Black colleagues don't need to.

Out of necessity, many of us have a personal set of unwritten rules we follow to exist safely. These are rules I have lived by and have discussed on numerous occasions with other Black scientists. To the Black scientist: may you find validation from reading this. You are not alone and your experiences are real and important, despite what others may tell you. To those non-Black people who strive to be allies: this will help you understand the additional precautions your Black colleagues regularly take and help you find ways to share some of this emotional burden. We need allies to help build safe spaces. By preparing you to recognize threats and to know which actions to take, the list that follows can help you create a more inclusive scientific community.

BLACK RULE #1: KNOW IT ALL, PROVE IT REPEATEDLY

Everyone faces stereotype threats—the need to avoid confirming negative stereotypes about your identity. For example, a NowThis video where I spoke about the importance of diversity in marine science garnered a large number of comments referring to stereotypes of Black people, including "Black people are afraid of water," "Black people aren't good at science and math," and my personal favorite, "Black people are too busy playing basketball." Black people are often stereotyped as being lazy and unintelligent. And, similar to the response to my video, this stereotype is often argued as the "reasoning" behind the lack of representation of Black folks in STEM careers.

As a result, Black scientists, like other Black professionals, are not given the benefit of the doubt and are held to a much more rigorous standard than others. To be taken seriously in science settings, we feel the pressure to perform flawlessly. We memorize every procedure and double- and triple-check every analysis to ensure that our work is beyond reproach. This stereotype threat says: You don't have to be the best to be a scientist... unless you're Black, and then you must be perfect. Allies can actively counter biases by leveraging their privilege and power to fight against oppressive systems.

Tips for allies:

Hype us up. Often, the extra energy and time we put into our work goes unnoticed.

Step out of the limelight. Black people's mistakes are often heavily criticized, while successes often go unacknowledged. Allies can combat this injustice by ensuring criticism is infrequent, always constructive, and framed in the context of a specific goal. If you can see you are getting overly praised while your Black colleague is continually criticized for doing the same caliber of work, consider taking a step back to address and acknowledge the biases that may be at play and turn the limelight on your Black colleague.

Don't assume incompetence. Ask if the Black scientist needs help, wants some tips, or has questions, remaining aware of your own knowledge boundaries. If you find yourself assuming Black scientists don't know what they're doing, be gentle and honest as you check for biases. Do you assume everyone who comes into that space doesn't know what they're doing, or some over others?

Create a space for questions. Don't answer questions in a condescending tone, and make sure you are constructive and not overly critical. Provide actionable advice to reach an explicit goal and mention if you have ever had similar questions. No one likes to be judged for asking a question.

Volunteer. In an effort to combat the "lazy" stereotype, Black scientists often take on more roles, responsibilities, and service positions than their non-Black colleagues. On top of that, these additional roles are often undervalued, and they often don't get compensated fairly or at all. You can combat this pattern by volunteering to do some of the undesirable or less glamorous work and advocating for fair pay to support the additional roles your colleague has undertaken.

Learn about white supremacy culture. Check out works by Kenneth Jones and Tema Okun that teach the characteristics of white supremacy culture and how to identify and address them in your workspaces.

BLACK RULE #2: NEVER LET THEM SEE YOU SWEAT

Following up on rule #1, stereotype threat isn't just an issue in academia but in our interpersonal relationships too. Black scientists may face injustices, microaggressions, and exclusionary behavior from our colleagues, and speaking up is often a measured risk. Black people are often stereotyped as "angry," and taking a strong stance in a situation may lead to tone policing—deflecting to the emotion of an argument to avoid addressing the content—or retaliation—poor or aggressive treatment in direct response to opposing discrimination. Special care is required in the face of these harmful behaviors to decide which interpersonal issues are worth fighting for. When we do decide to speak out for our needs, we battle the pressure to remain calm, unreactive, and poised, lest we be accused of overreacting, acting "ghetto," or causing a scene. Even when we have a right to be upset, our anger could be used against us. Allies can help dissipate the burdens by publicly agreeing with us and supporting or amplifying our voices when we bring attention to issues in personal and professional settings.

Tips for allies:

When addressed, focus on content, not tone. When colleagues address a concern, focus on what they are saying; that's what should be addressed. If concerns come up about approach, create a separate time to discuss it; do not derail.

Be an advocate. You may have more ability to lodge a complaint than your Black colleagues. Get their approval, then bring up the issue or address the problem so that it gets addressed without them having to carry the emotional weight.

De-escalate. When issues get brought up, a Black person often will get blamed for creating it. When advocating for someone, pay attention to their body language and follow their lead. You are there for support and to amplify their voice, so be sure to listen carefully. Nonviolent communication is a tool for de-escalation that consists of making observations without evaluation, feeling empathy, recognizing needs, and making clear and honest requests. The Center for Nonviolent Communication has great resources for those interested in improving interpersonal relationships.

BLACK RULE #3: TAKE A WHITE FRIEND

Some spaces can be a risk to Black scientists' physical or emotional safety. In these situations, it can be helpful to bring a white ally who we trust to be an active bystander by de-escalating tense situations, recording when necessary, speaking with police or authority figures, and using their privilege to protect us when needed. Simply the presence of a white body can be an effective tool in assisting Black people with de-escalation efforts by confronting stereotypes driven by white supremacy with something white supremacy cannot ignore: whiteness. Finding a willing white ally, however, can be difficult. In this deep level of allyship, we put a lot of trust in this person to believe us, protect us, and defend us if necessary.

Tips for allies:

Stick like glue. Your biggest responsibility is to communicate with your Black colleague about their needs and help with their needs as much as possible, whether that's to stay with them the whole time, check in regularly, or stay within earshot.

Believe them. From years of experience, many Black folks develop a kind of sixth sense—like Spider-Man's "spidey sense"—for impending danger and racist threats. You may not see a problem because you have had a different life experience. But if a Black colleague tells you, "We need to go," you go. If they say, "Don't stop at that gas station," don't stop. If they say, "Don't call the police for help," trust them. Being an ally means sometimes having to pull the plug on an experiment or change study sites because your colleague's safety is more important than data.

Avoid, deflect, and defend. By following the first two tips as well as doing your own research to ensure you are going somewhere safe for all of your colleagues, you will avoid conflicts, but conflicts may still arise. As an ally, your job is to practice the four active bystander techniques: direct action, distraction, delegation, and delay. You need to communicate with, listen to, and read the body language of your colleague to make sure you can step in when they need you to. When asked, you should do the talking when speaking to authority figures or those with disproportionate power (for example, law enforcement or "Karens"). In extreme conflict, you may need to form a physical barrier between the threat and your colleague, or you may have to document wrongdoing with your phone. Either way, it is important to understand that it may take effort on your part. Whatever risk you assume, however, is likely much lower than the risk your Black colleague faces.

BLACK RULE #4: AVOID THE HOTEL BAR

At a conference when the talks have finished up for the day, folks often head to the hotel bar to relax and unwind, but Black scientists may remain tense because alcohol can heighten dangers. Marginalized people, including Black people and women (this goes double if you're a Black woman, like me), are often more heavily judged for their alcohol consumption than their white male counterparts. Balancing this with wanting to—as the character Aaron Burr says in the musical *Hamilton*—"be in the room where it happens" can make Black scientists feel like they are walking a tightrope. Should we be included in conversations or on professional outings, or should we avoid activities we could be judged for?

Social drinking disinhibits people, and some may behave poorly under its influence, carrying out microaggressions, sexual harassment, racist remarks, and bullying. Frequently people think they can blame it on the alcohol, but alcohol doesn't magically make someone racist—the blame falls solely on the perpetrator. Many Black scientists may avoid social drinking events or instead remain sober. Of course, many others avoid drinking alcohol for a variety of personal and/or religious reasons. Avoiding the bar, however, can make it more difficult to break into the "old boys' club" because many bonds and collaborations are formed over beers, as unhealthy as this connection with alcohol may be.

Tips for allies:

Create and attend alcohol-free events. Break the unhealthy connection to alcohol and host events like tea times, mocktail hours, picnics, game nights, and such.

Call out harmful behaviors. If you hear or see someone step out of line, hold them accountable. Watch out for those around you and intervene when necessary to get folks to a safe location.

BLACK RULE #5: CODE SWITCH . . . OR DON'T!

One of my biggest challenges in professional settings is how I communicate my thoughts. The dialect of my South Carolinian family and those I grew up with in the South is not expected or accepted in science spaces. I think it's absurd, as dialect doesn't imply intelligence, but people often equate African American Vernacular English and Southern twangs with ignorance. Language and honest representation that bucks the system are at the forefront of many Black scientists' minds. Code switching means changing the way someone talks to fit the dialect of those around them. Like the previous rules, this is not hard and fast; it depends on the person, the setting, and the moment. There is no right or wrong way. There is only what is best for you at that moment.

Tips for allies:

Meet us halfway. If someone chooses not to code switch in your presence, they likely deem you a safe person who isn't going to judge them for the way they express themselves. To show respect, let them have this brief respite. You may not speak their language, but you should attempt to understand it. This might mean doing your own research, asking questions, or paying attention to context clues, as you would with any other language.

Don't make it a big thing. Pointing out or judging words or phrases can make someone feel as if their full selves aren't welcome in a space. It's okay for language to be unfamiliar to you; it is not "weird" or "ghetto" or "wrong." Check your biases and remain respectful.

For the love of all things holy, *don't use a "blaccent"* (fake an African American Vernacular dialect). Don't do it, just don't. African American Vernacular is a dialect that was created as a result of forcibly displaced Africans from various countries coming together and collectively learning English, a language that was never taught to them, and making a beautiful mosaic of language. Using it as slang without recognizing it as a true and valid language disrespects this legacy.

Black scientists want nothing more than to just be scientists, mind our own business, and live our lives. We all want to live in a world where we don't have to consider these risks, where Blackness is natural in scientific and outdoor spaces, but we must acknowledge reality for our collective well-being. Until we reach parity, these rules of engagement can help us maintain our mental and physical wellness and safety. Many of these practices add labor and stress to an already stressful career; choosing when to balance our personal safety with building a better world and fighting the system can be confusing and emotionally taxing. Allies who alleviate the burden can make a world of difference as we strive to be as unencumbered as our white counterparts.

ALL I EVER NEEDED

Dr. Tiara Moore

The biggest letdown was getting my PhD. I thought that even though I might be the only Black person in the room, I would at least **belong** in the room. I'm a marine scientist so I never expected labs or conferences to be filled with Black people, but I also never expected to be treated as if I didn't belong or have lab doors slammed in my face or be asked questions like "Oh, you can swim?!" or "You get your hair wet?" For some reason I thought I would finally be seen. But naw, I was wrong. Not only was there no sense of belonging in that room, I could tell I was never wanted in that room. It was an all-too-familiar feeling, one I had spent most of my life running from.

See, before I was even born, I wasn't wanted. My grandmother overheard my seventeen-year-old mother's call to a clinic and canceled her appointment. It was a story I should never have heard, and it birthed a longing for acceptance and a hope for anyone or anything to want me. Even though my mom kept me, just before my second birthday she was incarcerated. My father was young and jobless, and he didn't fight for me, so my grandmother was granted custody of me. Somebody wanted me, I thought.

It was a full house and my grandmother was a single parent. My mom and grandmother were young parents and my grandmother was still having children after I was born, meaning I have two aunts who are younger than me. There were a lot of mouths to feed, so whenever there were money struggles, I was immediately told I was the problem, or if the kids wanted something we couldn't afford, it was blamed on me. Growing up, I often heard statements like "Well, you know T is here, and she has to eat too," which made me feel like a burden to my grandmother and a problem for her children. They hated that they couldn't have the life they wanted because of me, so they would tease me about my mom and even made up a little song to taunt me, "That's why your mama in jaillll!" Repeatedly they would sing the song and let me know they didn't want me around, so I felt like an outsider inside of this place I called home. It made me want to do everything I could to leave, to have a better life, to figure out a way to be a person people would want. So I became an overachiever.

Whatever it was, I had to do it to the extreme. I had to read the most books in elementary school and become the number one accelerated reader. Do y'all remember the Pizza Hut BOOK IT! program? I got the most free personal pizzas from Pizza Hut, my favorite thing to eat—pepperoni, to be exact. Sometimes I would collect the coupons or get more than one pizza and share them with my aunts to make them be nice to me. Reading was my escape from my reality, so I read a lot. I did everything a lot. I went out of my way to help people everywhere I went. I had to be the best at everything so I could help with everything. I wanted people to need my help. Then they would want me. I wanted people to be proud of me.

If I was good at things, I would finally be wanted. Somehow, being an overachiever would make my dad want to be my dad. Maybe if he had known what a good person I would turn out to be, he would have fought harder to keep me. He would be so proud of his little accelerated reader, he would want me. That's how that works, right? I thought so, so I continued trying to find ways to stand out. I decided to become the first in my family to finish college and go to medical school to become a pediatrician.

In college, I became curious about other biology courses and signed up for a tropical biology class. I'll be honest, I signed up only because they were going to Costa Rica for spring break, so I was like, "Free trip, yesss!" But when we arrived, it was beyond what I could have expected. I spent a week on a boat collecting ocean water samples and doing exciting water quality experiments to check for pollution, and there were senior scientists helping us along. I remember asking them, "Is this a job? Are y'all getting paid for this?" That's how I found out about marine science, not only as a career but also as an entire lifetime of adventure.

When I was a kid, we made the four-hour drive to the beach maybe three times, and I spent a few Saturdays at Lake Greenwood in high school, but I didn't really have a connection to water. The beach and the ocean were just there, a place Black people seemingly didn't really mess with. In my experience, they existed for lounging and taking photos. This new idea of spending my career exploring the ocean was thrilling, and I found out I could still be a doctor but of marine science. I didn't need an MD, I was gonna have a PhD instead! I just knew becoming a bad-ass marine scientist would make people proud of me and definitely make my parents want me.

After that life-changing Costa Rica trip, I started looking for graduate school programs in marine science. I had attended a predominantly white institution to earn my bachelor of science in biology. I wanted to switch it up for my master's and attend a historically Black college or university (HBCU) for grad school. I didn't realize how hard it would be to find a marine science program at an HBCU, but Hampton University in Virginia fit the bill. At Hampton, my research focused on linking human impacts to the decline of water quality in Chesapeake Bay. I spent even more time on more boats, did more experiments, and spoke at scientific conferences. After I graduated, I became a scientific scuba diver and traveled the world exploring coral reefs, assessing biodiversity in the face of climate change, as part of a diversity program aimed at giving Black students international research experiences. I was finally in a space where I felt people wanted me to be there, so I continued on to get my PhD. Fast-forward six years, and I'm finally Dr. Moore; my parents are proud of me and I feel like I belong, like I have finally arrived! I'm a full-time scientist working in a lab doing research that I love.

Still, after working so hard to get there, the experience wasn't what I expected.

I knew going in that marine science is a predominantly white field, but at the PhD level and in the Pacific Northwest, it is white white, which was isolating. Walking into the building, lab, or lunch area meant facing "You can't sit with me" vibes. I mean, I was sometimes the only Black person I would see all day, and it was unexpectedly lonely. I'd go to the bathroom, look in the mirror, and say, "Hey girl!" just to have someone to chat with. These spaces were also unwelcoming. People treated me like I didn't belong, by leaving me off emails, refusing to order my lab supplies, or literally slamming doors in my face. There were daily microaggressions and then gaslighting when I brought it up. It was, "Oh, they never treat meeeeeee like that, I'm sure you're mistaken." Or "I'm sure they didn't mean it, they're greeaaat." *OK, Tony the Tiger.*

Constantly battling with feeling unwelcome and unsupported, I found myself questioning my purpose. My mental health started to suffer. Those feelings from my past of being unwanted started rising back to the surface. My thoughts grew dark. *Will anyone ever want me around? Do I belong anywhere? Should I quit science? Should I quit life?* I lost interest in my research. I found myself showing up to work meetings but never interacting, a shell. Eventually, I stopped going. I was in crisis; I couldn't figure out my next move. Then the murders of Breonna Taylor and George Floyd happened. My world was shaken and again changed forever.

On a large scale, I saw how Black people were not wanted in America. We were seen as the people who didn't belong, predators whose necks needed to be stomped on. That damning feeling of not being wanted or welcomed was triggered, and my heart broke. I asked myself, *How can people treat people like this? Will we ever belong? Will we ever be protected? Will we ever be wanted?* As these tragedies were occurring, we were also trapped inside due to the global COVID-19 pandemic, so a lot of these events were largely seen and experienced over social media. This amplified the feelings of isolation but also created a sense of community among Black people across the world. We all wanted to be heard, we all wanted justice, we all wanted to be wanted. Most important, we wanted the racial harassment to stop, but it didn't. Through social media we got to witness how Black people weren't wanted even in places like Central Park, and that ended up causing yet another shift in my own story.

The fallout from Christian Cooper's harassment struck a nerve in the Black birding community (yes, it exists), and with the first-ever Black Birders Week, its members began dispelling the myth that Black people don't bird-watch. Now y'all, this was a week of virtual events, and Black birders around the globe posted photos of themselves frolicking in nature, looking at birds. I was scrolling on Twitter like, "Well, will you look at thissss!" They had panels and workshops all highlighting Black people bird-watching to normalize Black birders and prevent future harassment like that in Central Park.

Black Birders Week got the other STEM fields looking like, "Hold up, wait, it's Black people ova here too!!" and more themed "Black In" weeks started popping up. There is now an annual Black in Physics Week, Black in Neuro Week, Black in Geoscience Week, Black in Astro Week, Black in Botany Week, and many more, each using its platform to amplify the Black voices in predominantly white fields. It was an electrifying movement that changed how people see Black people and how people see scientists. Feeling left out, I tweeted, "Hol up, where is Black in Marine Science Week at?!" I couldn't have imagined the response.

In twenty-four hours the tweet had hundreds of likes and comments from marine scientists around the world wanting to help me plan the week! I went from just tweeting to "Oh damn, I have to do some work now." From the comments and follow-up conversations, I pulled together an organizing team with both Black marine scientists and allies from the field who didn't identify as Black but wanted to support Black in Marine Science (BIMS) Week. In about three months, we created a logo, started social media channels, raised more than $25,000 in funds, and planned the first week dedicated to Black people in marine science.

Through the week, more than three hundred scientists introduced themselves using #BIMSRollCall on social media, and we had more than three thousand participants attend our events virtually. We had panels on scuba diving while Black and taking care of our natural hair. We found healing as we shared our experiences with racism and power, knowing we were no longer alone. I realized in that moment that while we may be the only Black person in our room, there are hundreds of rooms, so it's hundreds of us. I planned to find us all. BIMS Week left me feeling hopeful—it was one of those feelings that shakes you up and makes you want to change everything. I had to bottle this feeling up; I couldn't let it get away. I had to find a way to get more funding and make it bigger; I had to overachieve.

I decided to create an organization dedicated to celebrating the work of Black marine scientists, spreading environmental awareness, and inspiring the next generation of scientific thought leaders. After receiving some sizable donations, I registered Black in Marine Science (BIMS) as a nonprofit organization. BIMS is the beginning of a pipeline, supporting Black marine scientists from kindergarten all the way to university professor and beyond. With BIMS, I am creating places of belonging for innovative marine science research and increasing ocean science literacy in Black communities. We now have a thriving YouTube channel, BIMSTV, filled with educational content for all ages. We already have more than two hundred episodes of Black marine scientists sharing their research and making it accessible to all. We run programs that remove the financial barriers to becoming scuba divers. I speak on panels and give talks across the world about the lack of diversity in marine science, providing my experiences and opinions as tools to make the field better, and I get paid for it, honey.

Building Black in Marine Science saved my life, and it all started from a single tweet. We have created safe spaces to discuss racial harassment and provide solutions for healing and action. We have become the space I always wished I had. I'm literally the change I wanted to see. The heartbreak I felt after getting my PhD and still not feeling wanted or welcome is still with me, but I'm finally starting to heal and find my place in this thing called life. Most important, I finally feel wanted. People want me to lead them, want me to come talk and give advice, and want to help me with my vision for Black in Marine Science.

Next I want to build our own research and outreach facility called the BIMS Institute. It will be a world-renowned innovative research powerhouse, the first of its kind and led entirely by Black marine scientists. We will have students and members of the community included in all of our research projects, and we will make sure everyone always has access to the data we are gathering. It will be my life's work. I can't wait for the day when I'm standing in front of the BIMS Institute right after our ribbon-cutting opening. I'll walk to the door of the Moore Lab and sit in that room, realizing all I ever needed was me.

ACKNOWLEDGMENTS

The creators of this book would like to thank our land and blood ancestors for helping shape our planet and our paths. We acknowledge our severance from our history and our forced placement on unceded, settled land. We especially honor the Ute, Cheyenne, Arapahoe (of present-day Boulder, Colorado); Tutelo/Monacan, Cherokee, and Yuchi peoples (of present-day southwest Virginia); and the Duwamish, Suquamish, Muckleshoot peoples (of present-day Seattle).

We extend deep gratitude toward our blood and found families and our friends for their feedback and ongoing support. We could not have made this book without you!

We also send deepest thanks to Kate Rogers, Laura Shauger, Lorraine Anderson, Jen Grable, and the rest of the publication team at Mountaineers Books for forming this project and guiding our way. Thank you for all your hard work and brilliance!

RESOURCES

This extensive list includes everything from publications mentioned in this collection, to areas of environmental science some contributors are researching, to the history of racism and discrimination in the outdoors. We recommend that you chip away at this abundant information over time, as you feel inclined to broaden your perspective.

REFERENCES

Arancibia, Daniel, Steven Farber, Beth Savan, Yvonne Verlinden, Nancy Smith Lea, Jeff Allen, and Lee Vernich. "Measuring the Local Economic Impacts of Replacing On-Street Parking with Bike Lanes." *Journal of the American Planning Association* 85, no. 4 (2019): 463–81. doi.org/10.1080/01944363.2019.1638816.

Axleson Gustave. "5 Key Lessons to Take Home from the First #BlackBirdersWeek." *All About Birds*. June 2020, allaboutbirds.org/news/5-key-lessons-to-take-home-from-the-first-blackbirdersweek.

Carney, Judith A. "'With Grains in Her Hair': Rice in Colonial Brazil." *Slavery & Abolition* 25, no. 1 (2004): 1–27. doi.org/10.1080/0144039042000220900.

Ellis, Erle C., Nicolas Gauthier, Kees Klein Goldewijk, Rebecca Bliege Bird, Nicole Boivin, Sandra Díaz, Dorian Q. Fuller, Jacquelyn L. Gill, Jed O. Kaplan, Naomi Kingston, et al. "People Have Shaped Most of Terrestrial Nature for at Least 12,000 Years." *Proceedings of the National Academy of Sciences* 118, no. 17 (2021). doi.org/10.1073/pnas.2023483118.

Fortin, Jacey. "She Was the Only Woman in a Photo of 38 Scientists, and Now She's Been Identified." *New York Times*, March 19, 2018, nytimes.com/2018/03/19/us/twitter-mystery-photo.html.

"Gender Expansive, Genderqueer, Gender Nonconforming (GE, Gi)." It Gets Better, December 23, 2021. itgetsbetter.org/glossary/gender-nonconforming/.

LaFrance, Adrienne. "How the Bicycle Paved the Way for Women's Rights." *The Atlantic*, June 26, 2014. theatlantic.com/technology/archive/2014/06/the-technology-craze-of-the-1890s-that-forever-changed-womens-rights/373535/.

Maathai, Wangari. *The Green Belt Movement: Sharing the Approach and the Experience.* New York: Lantern Books, 2006.

McGlashen, Andy. "Getting to Know Jerome Ford, the Government's Top Bird Official." *Audubon News*, April 2, 2021. audubon.org/news/getting-know-jerome-ford-governments-top-bird-official.

Miles, Tiya. "Every Pecan Tree: Trees, Meaning, and Memory in Enslaved People's Lives." Arnold Arboretum, Harvard University, April 9, 2021. youtube/LOcEU1iPoYY.

"Multi-State: Trail of Tears National Historic Trail (US National Park Service)." Washington, DC: Department of the Interior. Accessed January 31, 2023. nps.gov/articles/trailoftears.htm.

Nodjimbadem, Katie. "The Lesser-Known History of African-American Cowboys." *Smithsonian Magazine*, February 13, 2017. smithsonianmag.com/history/lesser-known-history-african-american-cowboys-180962144/

Popova, Maria, "Wheels of Change: How the Bicycle Empowered Women." *The Atlantic*, March 28, 2011. theatlantic.com/technology/archive/2011/03/wheels-of-change-how-the-bicycle-empowered-women/73102.

Rowland-Shea, Jenny, Sahir Doshi, Shanna Edberg, and Robert Fanger. "*The Nature Gap*." Center for American Progress, July 21, 2020. americanprogress.org/article/the-nature-gap.

Schaefer, Jaclyn S., Miguel A. Figliozzi, and Avinash Unnikrishnan. "Evidence from Urban Roads without Bicycle Lanes on the Impact of Bicycle Traffic on Passenger Car Travel Speeds." *Transportation Research Record* 2674 no. 7 (July 2020): 87–98. doi.org/10.1177/0361198120920880.

Shaffer, Earl V. *Walking with Spring: The First Thru-Hike of the Appalachian Trail*. Harpers Ferry, WV: Appalachian Trail Conference, 2004.

"Tanisha Williams: Botanist and Founder of Black Botanists Week." PBS Nature blog, February 11, 2021. pbs.org/wnet/nature.blog.

Weisstuch, Liza. "Harriet Tubman Is Famous for Being an Abolitionist and Political Activist, but She Was Also a Naturalist." *Smithsonian Magazine*, March 10, 2022. smithsonianmag.com/history/harriet-tubman-is-famous-for-being-an-abolitionist-and-political-activist-but-she-was-also-a-naturalist-180979689.

"Your 'Deadline' Won't Kill You—Or Will It?" Word History. *Merriam-Webster*. merriam-webster.com/words-at-play/your-deadline-wont-kill-you.

RECOMMENDED READING

BOOKS

Anderson, Carol. *White Rage*. London: Bloomsbury Publishing, 2016.

Anjani, Ashia. *Heirloom: Collected Poems*. Portland, Oregon: Write Bloody Publishing, 2023.

Belleny, Danielle. *This Is a Book for People Who Love Birds*. New York: Running Press, 2022.

Désir, Alison Mariella. *Running While Black: Finding Freedom in a Sport That Wasn't Built for Us*. New York: Penguin Random House, 2022.

Dungy, Camille T. *Black Nature: Four Centuries of African American Nature Poetry*. Athens: University of Georgia Press, 2009.

——. *Soil: The Story of a Black Mother's Garden*. New York: Simon & Schuster, 2023.

Finney, Carolyn. *Black Faces, White Spaces: Reimagining the Relationship of African Americans to the Great Outdoors*. Chapel Hill: University of North Carolina Press, 2014.

Flowers, Catherine Colman. *Waste: One Woman's Fight Against America's Dirty Secret*. New York: The New Press, 2022.

Graham, Jasmin, Camila Caceres, and Deborah Santos de Azevedo Menna. *Minorities in Shark Sciences: Diverse Voices in Shark Research*. Milton Park, Oxfordshire: Routledge, 2022.

Gumbs, Alexis Pauline. *Undrowned: Black Feminist Lessons from Marine Mammals*. Chico, CA: AK Press, 2020.

Hernandez, Jess. *Fresh Banana Leaves: Healing Indigenous Landscapes through Indigenous Science*. New York: Penguin Random House, 2022.

Kimmerer, Robin Wall. *Braiding Sweetgrass*. Minneapolis: Milkweed Editions, 2015.

Lanham, J. Drew. *The Home Place: Memoirs of a Colored Man's Love Affair with Nature*. Minneapolis: Milkweed Editions, 2017.

Loach, Mikaela. *It's Not That Radical: Climate Action to Transform Our World*. London: Dorling Kindersley, 2023.

Lugo, Derick. *The Unlikely Thru-Hiker: An Appalachian Trail Journey*. Boston: Appalachian Mountain Club Books, 2019.

Mapp, Rue. *Nature Swagger: Stories and Visions of Black Joy in the Outdoors*. San Francisco: Chronicle Books, 2022. Featuring a story by Leandra Taylor.

Miles, Tiya. *All That She Carried: The Journey of Ashley's Sack, A Black Family Keepsake*. New York: Penguin Random House, 2021.

Mills, James Edward. *The Adventure Gap: Changing the Face of the Outdoors*. Seattle: Mountaineers Books, 2014.

Harris, J. Robert. *Way Out There: Adventures of a Wilderness Trekker*. Seattle: Mountaineers Books, 2017.

Johnson, Ayana Elizabeth, and Katharine K. Wilkinson. *All We Can Save: Truth, Courage, and Solutions for the Climate*. New York: One World, 2021.

Opoku-Agyeman, Anna Gifty. *The Black Agenda: Bold Solutions for a Broken System*. New York: St. Martin's Press, 2022.

Penniman, Leah. *Black Earth Wisdom: Soulful Conversations with Black Environmentalist*. New York: HarperCollins, 2023.

———. *Farming While Black: Soul Fire Farm's Practical Guide to Liberation on the Land*. White River Junction, VT: Chelsea Green Publishing, 2018.

Savoy, Lauret. *Trace: Memory, History, Race, and the American Landscape*. Berkeley, CA: Counterpoint Press, 2015.

Sharkey, Erin. *A Darker Wilderness: Black Nature Writing from Soil to Stars*. Minneapolis: Milkweed Editions, 2023.

Thomas, Leah. *The Intersectional Environmentalist: How to Dismantle Systems of Oppression to Protect People + Planet*. New York: Voracious, 2022.

ARTICLES

Bashir, Asma. "Scientist or Artist? How I Realized I Don't Have to Choose." *Science Magazine*, April 28, 2022. science.org/content/article/scientist-or-artist-how-i-realized-i-don-t-have-choose.

Benson, Emily. "#BlackBirdersWeek Takes on Systemic Racism." *High Country News*, June 1, 2020. hcn.org/issues/52.7/north-race-and-racism-blackbirdersweek-takes-on-systemic-racism-by-celebrating-diversity. Featuring Sheridan Alford.

Bereger, Erin. "How Earyn McGee Sent the Internet Searching for Lizards." *Outside*, January 23, 2022, outsideonline.com/culture/books-media/earyn-mcgee-herpetologist-twitter-find-that-lizard.

Bert, Allison. "On Being LGBTQ+ in Science—Yes It Matters, and Here's Why." *Elsevier Connect*, July 25, 2019. elsevier.com/connect/on-being-lgbtq-in-science-yes-it-matters-and-heres-why. Featuring Dr. Alex Moore.

Eaglesnest. "The Story Behind the Outdoor Afro X ENO Kili Mapp Kili DoubleNest Print Hammock." *ENO News*, June 15, 2021. eaglesnestoutfittersinc.com/blogs/news/the-story-behind-the-outdoor-afro-x-eno-kili-mapp-kili-doublenest-print-hammock. Featuring Leandra Taylor.

Finney, Carolyn. "Who Gets Left Out of the 'Great Outdoors' Story?" *New York Times*, November 4, 2021. nytimes.com/2021/11/04/style/black-outdoors-wilderness.html.

"Five Ways to Make the Outdoors More Inclusive." *Atlantic Re:think*, 2018. theatlantic.com/sponsored/rei-2018/five-ways-to-make-the-outdoors-more-Inclusive/3019.

Haile, Rahawa. "How Black Books Lit My Way along the Appalachian Trail," *Buzzfeed News*, Feburary 2, 2017, buzzfeednews.com/article/rahawahaile/how-black-books-lit-my-way-along-the-appalachian-trail.

Halsey, Samniqueka J., Lynette R. Strickland, Maya Scott-Richardson, Tolulope Perrin-Stowe, and Lynnicia Massenburg. "Elevate, Don't Assimilate, to Revolutionize the Experience of Ecologists and Evolutionary Biologists Who Are Black, Indigenous, and People of Colour," *Nature Ecology & Evolution* 4 (August 20, 2020): 1291–93. nature.com/articles/s41559-020-01297-9.

Indigenous Stewardship Methods and Natural Resources Conservation Practices Guidebook. Washington, DC: USDA, July 2010. efotg.sc.egov.usda.gov/references/public/va/IndigenousStewardship.pdf.

Lyons, Casey. "Birding While Black." *Backpacker Magazine*, June 4, 2020. backpacker.com/news-and-events/birding-while-black. Featuring Amber Wendler.

Mills, James Edward. "These People of Color Transformed US National Parks." *National Geographic*, August 5, 2020. nationalgeographic.com/travel/article/people-of-color-who-transformed-us-national-parks.

Miriti, Maria N., Karen Bailey, Samniqueka J. Halsey, and Nyeema C. Harris. "Hidden Figures in Ecology and Evolution." *Nature Ecology & Evolution* 4 (July 2020): 1282. nature.com/articles/s41559-020-1270-y.

Mohtasham, Diba, and Manoush Zomorodi. "Meet Alexis Nikole Nelson, the Wildly Popular 'Black Forager.'" *Code Switch*, NPR, September 9, 2021. www.npr.org/sections/codeswitch/2021/09/09/173838801/meet-alexis-nikole-nelson-the-wildly-popular-black-forager.

Moore, Tiara. "Viewpoint: The Only Black Person in the Room," *Association for the Sciences of Limnology and Oceanography*, November 2018. aslopubs.onlinelibrary.wiley.com/doi/pdf/10.1002/lob.10269.

Newsome, Melba. "Rising Seas Threaten the Gullah Geechee Culture: Here's How They're Fighting Back." *National Geographic*, July 2022. nationalgeographic.com/environment/article/rising-seas-threaten-the-gullah-geechee-culture-heres-how-theyre-fighting-back.

Roberts, Alexus, and Shaz Zamore, "Black in Nature." *Society for Integrative and Comparative Biology (blog)*, June 9, 2020. integrativeandcomparativebiology.wordpress.com/2020/06/09/black-in-nature.

"Stewardship Definitions." NOAA. Accessed October 2022. www.noaa.gov.

Steinmetz, Katy. "She Coined the Term 'Intersectionality' Over 30 Years Ago. Here's What It Means to Her Today." *Time Magazine*, February 20, 2020. time.com/5786710/kimberle-crenshaw-intersectionality.

VIDEOS AND FILMS

An American Ascent, anamericanascent.com
America Outdoors with Baratunde Thurston, PBS, pbs.org/show/america-outdoors-baratunde-thurston
Becoming Ruby, Patagonia, patagonia.com/stories/becoming-ruby/video-85848.html
Black Girl in the Woods, blackgirlinthewoods.org
Brotherhood of Skiing, REI, rei.com/blog/snowsports/rei-presents-brotherhood-of-skiing
Confronting Barriers in Conservation, Clark Dehart, Virginia Tech, featuring Sharon Dorsey, October 13, 2022, vtx.vt.edu/videos/k/2022/10/1_9x6mch8t.html
Extraordinary Birder with Christian Cooper, National Geographic Wild, 2023.

First-Time Birders: Birding 101 with Sheridan Alford, PBS, pbs.org/video/first-time-birders-birding-101-with-sheridan-alford-m82u2n.
Powerlands, powerlands.org/#:~:text=POWERLANDS-,Play,Indigenous%20activists%20across%20three%20continents
Reel Rock: Black Ice, Red Bull, redbull.com/us-en/episodes/reel-rock-s7-e9
Tending the Wild, PBS, pbs.org/show/tending-wild
"This Woman Wants More People of Color in Shark Sciences," featuring Jasmin Graham, *Now This Earth,* youtube/K6ic4x8FVOo
Twirling Tech Goddess, meow.wf/ttg, LeeLee James
Wood Hood, campingtoconnect.com/wood-hood

PODCASTS AND MUSIC

Bird Note: Sheridan Alford on Birding and Mental Health, Bird Note, May 31, 2022, birdnote.org/listen/shows/sheridan-alford-birding-and-mental-health
Her Royal Science, featuring Dr. A. Bashir, herroyalscience.com
"Forensic Ecology (Nature Detective) with Dr. Tiara Moore," Ologies, alieward.com/ologies/forensicecology
"Going Wild with Dr. Rae Wynn-Grant," *Nature,* PBS, pbs.org/wnet/nature/podcast/
The Trail Ahead, Faith E. Briggs and Addie Thompson, trailaheadpodcast.com
"Tree Song," *Today Is a Great Day!,* an album by Kelly Greenlight Thomas, music.youtube.com/watch?v=fvs8jFhxV5E
We Out Here, Alexi Grousis and Allison Jones, podcasts.apple.com/us/podcast/the-we-out-here-podcast/id1605379332

MAPS

African Diaspora Genomic Map, University of Colorado Anschutz Medical Campus, news.cuanschutz.edu/news-stories/scientists-map-genome-african-diaspora-americas
Appalachian Trail Interactive Map, appalachiantrail.org/explore/hike-the-a-t/interactive-map
Map of Africa, Interactive, Harvard Center for Geographic Analysis, Hutchins Center for African & African American Research, Harvard University, hutchinscenter.fas.harvard.edu/africamapworldmap-project
Native Land Map, Native Land Digital, native-land.ca
Trail of Tears Historic Trail Map, NPS, nps.gov/trte/planyourvisit/maps.htm
Underground Railroad Map, NPS, nps.gov/articles/000/iugrrm-mapping.htm

ORGANIZATIONS FEATURED IN STORIES

Bay Area Outreach and Recreation Program (borp.org) aims to improve the health, independence and social integration of children, youth, and adults with physical disabilities and visual impairments through sports, fitness, and recreation programs. BORP operates an adaptive bicycling-share program in partnership with Bay Wheels.
BlackAFinSTEM (blackafinstem.com) is a collective formed by the organizing members of **Black Birders Week**, BlackAFinSTEM seeks to support, uplift, and amplify Black STEM professionals in natural resources and the environment through professional development, career connection, and community engagement. BlackAFinSTEM organizes and hosts Black Birders Week annually.
Black Arts Retreat (blackartsretreat.com) is a home for Black creativity: providing restorative experiences that connect participants to art, whole wellness, nature, themselves

and each other. Black Arts Retreat provides a spirited environment where people connect with African Diasporic creative tools as a means of transforming their daily living.

Black in Marine Science (blackinmarinescience.org) is a community of Black marine scientists who highlight and amplify Black voices while inspiring younger generations through events, videos, and social engagement.

Black in Neuro (blackinneuro.com) strives to build a more diverse community with neuroscience-related fields and empower Black scholars and professionals via social media and events.

Black Joy on Wheels (blackjoyparade.org) is a hyper-positive nonprofit based in Oakland, California, that celebrates the Black experience and community's contribution to history and culture with its signature parade and celebration, partnerships, and events.

The Center for Nonviolent Communication (cnvc.org) is a global organization that supports the learning and sharing of nonviolent communication (NVC) and helps people peacefully and effectively resolve conflicts in personal, organizational, and political settings.

Dismantling Racism Works Web Workbook (dismantlingracism.org) is a web-based workbook originally designed to support the Dismantling Racism Works basic workshop developed by Kenneth Jones and Tema Okun.

(divorcing) White Supremacy Culture (whitesupremacyculture.info) is a website designed by Tema Okun to remix her widely circulated article, "White Supremacy Culture," which was written and published in 1999.

Landback (landback.org) is a movement that has existed for generations with a long legacy of organizing and sacrifice to get Indigenous lands back into Indigenous hands. These battles are being fought all across Turtle Island, to the north and south.

Melanin Base Camp (melaninbasecamp.com) aims to increase the visibility of outdoorsy Black, Indigenous, people of color to increase our representation in the media, advertising, and in the stories we tell ourselves about the outdoors.

Meow Wolf (meowwolf.com) is an arts and entertainment company based in Santa Fe, New Mexico, that creates immersive and interactive experiences to transport audiences of all ages into fantastic realms of story and exploration.

Minorities in Shark Sciences (misselasmo.org), started by four Black female shark researchers, promotes diversity and inclusion in shark science and encourages gender minorities of color to push through barriers and contribute knowledge in marine science.

The Noise Project (noiseproject.org) is a community science research project led by Kenneth Jones and Tema Okun. Funded by the National Science Foundation, the project is led by communities that have historically been excluded from the sciences.

Outdoor Afro (outdoorafro.org) is a network that celebrates and inspires Black connections and leadership in nature and connects Black people with our lands, water, and wildlife through outdoor education, recreation, and conservation.

Vision Zero Network (visionzeronetwork.org) is a strategy to eliminate all traffic fatalities and severe injuries, while increasing safe, healthy, equitable mobility for all.

OTHER ORGANIZATIONS WORTH CHECKING OUT

A WOC Space, awocspace.com, founded by Dr. Tiara Moore
Academics for Black Survival and Wellness, academics4blacklives.com
Amplify the Future, amplifythefuture.org
Backyard Basecamp, backyardbasecamp.org
Black Girl Environmentalist, blackgirlenvironmentalist.org
Black Girls Surf, blackgirlssurf.org

Black Girls Trekkin', blackgirlstrekkin.com
Black Folks Camp Too, blackfolkscamptoo.com
Black Kids Adventures, blackkidsadventures.org
Black Outside, blackoutside.org
Black Women in Ecology, Evolution, and Marine Science, bweems.org
Brown Girls Climb, browngirlsclimb.com
Earth in Color, earthincolor.co
Ebony Beach Club, ebonybeachclub.com, Natasha Smith
Environment for the Americas, environmentamericas.org
Field Inclusive, fieldinclusive.org
GirlTrek, girltrek.org
Greening Youth Foundation, gyfoundation.org
HBCUs Outside, hbcusoutside.com
The Humble Hustle Company, thehumblehustle.org, Sharon Dorsey, Leandra Taylor, and
    Amber Wendler
In Solidarity/Outdoor CEO Diversity Pledge, insolidarityproject.com
Latino Outdoors, latinooutdoors.org
Memphis Rox, memphisrox.org
Minority Outdoor Alliance, minorityoutdooralliance.org
Native Like Water, nativelikewater.org
Native Women's Wilderness, nativewomenswilderness.org
Paddle for Peace, paddleforpeace.org
Soul Trak, soultrak.com
STEMNoire, stemnoire.org
The Venture Out Project, ventureoutproject.com
Together Outdoors, togetheroutdoors.com
Unlikely Hikers, unlikelyhikers.org
Wild Diversity, wilddiversity.com

BLACK IN X WEEKS

For more Black in X Weeks, visit blackinx.org/community.
Black Birders Week, blackafinstem.com, including Sheridan Alford, Joelle Jenkins, Dakota
    Lane, Dr. Tiara Moore, Amber Wendler, Sidney Woodruff, and Dr. Shaz Zamore
Black Botanists Week, blackbotanistsweek.weebly.com, founded by Dr. Tanisha Williams
Black in Environment Week, blackinenviron.org, Sharon Dorsey
Black in Marine Science Week, blackinmarinescience.org, Jasmin Graham and Dr. Tiara
    Moore
Black in Neuro Week, blackinneuro.com, Dr. A. Bashir and Dr. Shaz Zamore

PLACES TO VISIT

African American Heritage Sites, located across the US, National Park Service, nps.gov/
    subjects/africanamericanheritage/visit.htm
The National Civil Rights Museum in Memphis, TN, civilrightsmuseum.org
National Museum of African American History and Culture in Washington, DC, nmaahc.
    si.edu
National Underground Railroad Freedom Center in Cincinnati, OH, freedomcenter.org
The Underground Railroad Bicycle Route, from Alabama to Ontario, adventurecycling.org/
    routes-and-maps/adventure-cycling-route-network/underground-railroad-ugrr/

ABOUT THE CONTRIBUTORS

Sheridan Alford is an environmental educator with a master's of natural resources in parks, recreation, and tourism management from the University of Georgia. Her fieldwork has taken her across the American South and led to work with PBS's *Nature*, Oboz Footwear, and others to enhance the minority experience in the outdoors. Sheridan has helped organize events and movements with the aim to elevate and support diversity in the birding community at large. Her focus includes citizen science, youth involvement, and the benefits of ecotherapy.

Dr. A. Bashir is a neuroscientist, spoken word artist, and host of *Her Royal Science*, a podcast she started while in graduate school to create safe spaces for individuals in STEM belonging to minoritized groups. She holds degrees from Boston University (BA, psychology) and the University of British Columbia (PhD, neuroscience). Dr. Bashir enjoys using writing as a form of catharsis and storytelling.

Sharon Dorsey is a graduate student at Virginia Tech studying shorebird ecology in Long Island, New York. While growing up in Baltimore, Maryland, she explored local parks and trails with her family, which encouraged her love for nature. Her mission is to show others in the Black community that they should be proud to be environmentalists and that historically, African Americans have fostered a relationship with nature through activities like farming, foraging, and fishing.

Avani Skye Fachon is an ecologist and multimedia storyteller. She holds a BA in ecology and evolutionary biology with a minor in media production from the University of Colorado, Boulder. Fachon is involved with several art-science projects, including Side by Side (www.sidebyside.world) and Rituals of This Good Earth (www.ritualsofthisgoodearth.com). She explores the intersection of ecological research, storytelling, and media-making to inspire problem-solving and collective action toward a more inclusive and sustainable future.

Dr. Karine A. Gibbs studies the social behaviors of tiny organisms. Her team asks how bacteria can recognize one another, form territories, and cause disease. Dr. Gibbs (AB, Harvard University; PhD, Stanford University) is an associate professor of plant and microbial biology at the University of California, Berkeley. She previously worked as an associate professor of molecular and cellular biology at Harvard. She enjoys running and bicycling as well as the conversations that can arise.

Jasmin Graham is president and CEO of Minorities in Shark Sciences (MISS), an organization dedicated to gender minorities of color in shark sciences. Graham is excited to help open doors for more underrepresented minority students to join the exciting field of marine science. Her work encompasses the areas of science communication, social justice, outreach, education, and conservation. She cares deeply about protecting endangered and vulnerable marine species, particularly elasmobranchs.

Dr. Samniqueka Halsey is an applied computational ecologist whose research stresses the importance of using long-term data sets, GIS, and remote sensing. Halsey uses computational approaches to understand the mechanisms involved in the patterns we see in nature. Outside of research, she enjoys adventure as much as staying at home reading a book. She has pushed her boundaries with traveling, camping, and hiking and vows to always try new experiences leading to self-discovery.

LeeLee James is channeling her engineering education, dance training, and resource-fulness through queer, femme, and Black identities into a wild and wonderful expression of her STEAM art through her YouTube series *Twirling Tech Goddess*. Having been a computer science major, James believes that greater access to technological information, skills, and experiences for those who have been historically marginalized is of the utmost importance in creating an equitable future for all. Learn more through her channel, meow.wf/ttg.

Joelle K. Jenkins is a socio-environmental scientist and graduate student researcher at the Ohio State University, studying environment and natural resources with an emphasis in environmental social science. Originally from Denver, Colorado, Jenkins has always taken pride in being Black in the outdoors. Her hobbies include birding, painting, dancing, singing, and more. With regard to her research, Jenkins is interested in improving the definition and practice of sustainability, while bridging the gap between racial equity and environmental impact assessments.

Dakota Lane is an undergraduate student in environmental science at Loyola University Chicago in the School of Environmental Sustainability. Her research as a John Grant Bioethics Fellow explores water ethics, sciences, and management through African diaspora cosmologies and knowledge systems. Born and raised on the Southside of Chicago, Lane focuses on the Chicago Area Waterway System and the Great Lakes region.

Dr. Alex Moore (she/they) is an assistant professor at the University of British Columbia in Vancouver. Raised in the Midwest, Dr. Moore spent the last decade in the Northeast completing graduate school, conducting environmental research, and being an advocate for diversity, equity, and inclusion in academia and conservation science. Now based in the Pacific Northwest, Dr. Moore hopes to continue advocating for communities of color and nature through teaching, research, and outreach.

Dr. Tiara Moore is a marine and environmental ecologist, the founder and CEO of Black in Marine Science, and the president of A WOC Space. A native of Greenwood, South Carolina, she has conducted research around the world assessing human impacts on biodiversity and water quality in coral reefs, estuaries, and forests. Inside and outside of the lab, Dr. Moore hopes her research in biodiversity will translate to increasing the overall diversity of perspectives in science.

Camille (Cam) Mosley is an avid outdoor adventurer and native of southern Mississippi. They are a PhD candidate studying recreational fisheries ecology at the University of Notre Dame. Mosley participates in various service roles both on and off campus. They received a BS in environmental science from Emory University and hope to highlight the contributions of the Black community to the environmental movement and research science. Mosley enjoys fishing, camping, cooking, and spending time with their loved ones.

Xorla Seyram Ocloo is an environmental social scientist earning a PhD in population biology, ecology, and evolution at Emory University. She received an MS from the University of Michigan and a BS from the University of Illinois, Urbana-Champaign. Ocloo believes in uplifting Black scholars in research and using transdisciplinary approaches to solve complex social and environmental problems. She hopes to inspire Black girls to live their authentic and confident selves.

Boluwatife Olawale is an Africa-based creative writer and content creator whose works have been featured in reputable literary journals, both locally and internationally. She desires to motivate Black people to appreciate the beauty of their origins and be selfless leaders through the art of writing. Her research interests are molecular biology, bioinformatics, and neuroscience. She is a research assistant at Helix Biogen Institute in Nigeria, where she is exploring the use of bioinformatics tools to develop a hantavirus vaccine.

Natasha Smith is an "unprofessional" athlete and member of the Ebony Beach Club, a group committed to introducing more Black people to the ocean through beach parties and surf lessons. An active surfer and traveler, she chases waves up and down the California coast in her van and regularly makes international trips to explore different cultures. Smith is passionate about teaching people that there are no age or cultural restrictions on being active in sports and activities. She enjoys surfing, motocross, skateboarding, mountain biking, and most other sports that involve motion.

Leandra Taylor is an artist, environmental scientist, and mountaineer based in Asheville, North Carolina. She grew up in Colorado Springs, Colorado, and was raised in a military family. Taylor discovered her love for science and nature at a young age and studied environmental science at Baylor University. She spends her time helping people connect with nature and sharing her love for hiking, bird-watching, and nature journaling.

Kelly GreenLight Thomas is a performance artist, educator, wellness warrior, and cultural organizer. For more than a decade, Thomas has been creating performance around emotional health, women's narratives, and nature. She is the foundress of @BlackArtsRetreat, an international hub for black creativity, culture, and holistic wellness.

Dr. Tanisha M. Williams is the Richard E. and Yvonne Smith Postdoctoral Fellow at Bucknell University. Dr. Williams earned a PhD in ecology and evolutionary biology from the University of Connecticut. Her dissertation research examined the impacts of climate change on South African flora, and her postdoctoral research elucidates the role Aboriginal Peoples play in the maintenance of Australian flora. She also uses genomics methods to update the conservation status of rare plants. Dr. Williams has extensive communication and policy experience and is the founder of Black Botanists Week.

Sidney Woodruff is a Black, biracial, and nonbinary PhD student in ecology at the University of California, Davis. Researching native turtle conservation, their work brings them to the outdoors to both learn and play. Woodruff's experiences breaking into the outdoor recreation world have made them passionate about mentorship, community building, and eliminating barriers to the sports and hobbies they pursue. Woodruff loves to spend time rock climbing, skiing, or looking for frogs and turtles.

ABOUT THE EDITORS

Amber Wendler (left) has a wide breadth of outdoor experiences from field research, outdoor education, volunteer work, and recreation that has taken her across the US and Latin America. Some of her favorite outdoor activities include running, backpacking, birdwatching, and kayaking. Wendler earned a BA in biology from Boston University and is a PhD candidate in biological sciences and Interfaces of

Global Change Fellow at Virginia Tech. She is passionate about making STEAM and the outdoors more inclusive through science communication and outreach. Find out what she's up to @AmberWendler on Instagram and Twitter.

Dr. Shaz Zamore (right) is a seasoned snowboarder, runner, and fire performer with a lifelong curiosity for animal behavior and biomechanical control. Zamore earned a BS in biological sciences from Cornell University and PhD in neuroscience from the University of Washington, studying sensory processing and behavior in organisms from tree swallows and rats to mosquitoes and flying snakes. Their fifteen-year practice in STEAM communication inspired their research project and business, Craniate, which creates culturally responsive neuroscience comics and experiment kits for marginalized learners. Find out what they're up to @TheDoctaZ on Instagram and Twitter.

GIVING BACK

The contributors to *Been Outside* believe it's important to support organizations working to share the outdoors and promote healthy living in local communities. Coeditors Amber Wendler and Shaz Zamore have partnered with Mountaineers Books to direct a portion of all royalties from sales of this book to support Humble Hustle.

The Humble Hustle Company (THHC), a local 501(c)(3) nonprofit organization based in Roanoke, Virginia, empowers Black youth and connects diverse communities by creating innovative, inclusive spaces that inspire hope and promote giving. THHC has several programs that expose, educate, and empower youth in the Roanoke community and surrounding areas like the Humble Hikes program that expands young peoples' horizons through outdoor activities, such as hiking, biking, and kayaking, and education in environmental science. The PRETTY Humble program cultivates and develops young Black women by empowering them through entrepreneurship, financial literacy, and leadership development.

THHC also runs The Collective, a creative and entrepreneurship hub that offers a platform that evokes out-of-the-box thinking to support hearts, minds, and souls. Humble Hustle gives back to the community through Keep Giving Initiatives for students: a Back to School Drive that supplies hygiene items and a Winter Coat Drive to help underpriviledged youth.

All in all, The Humble Hustle Company aims to inspire everyone to teach love and keep giving! Connect with them at www.thehumblehustle.org.

recreation · lifestyle · conservation

MOUNTAINEERS BOOKS, including its two imprints, Skipstone and Braided River, is a leading publisher of quality outdoor recreation, sustainability, and conservation titles. As a 501(c)(3) nonprofit, we are committed to supporting the environmental and educational goals of our organization by providing expert information on human-powered adventure, sustainable practices at home and on the trail, and preservation of wilderness.

Our publications are made possible through the generosity of donors, and through sales of 700 titles on outdoor recreation, sustainable lifestyle, and conservation. To donate, purchase books, or learn more, visit us online:

MOUNTAINEERS BOOKS
1001 SW Klickitat Way, Suite 201 • Seattle, WA 98134
800-553-4453 • mbooks@mountaineersbooks.org • www.mountaineersbooks.org

An independent nonprofit publisher since 1960

YOU MAY ALSO LIKE:

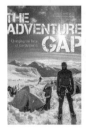

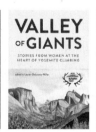